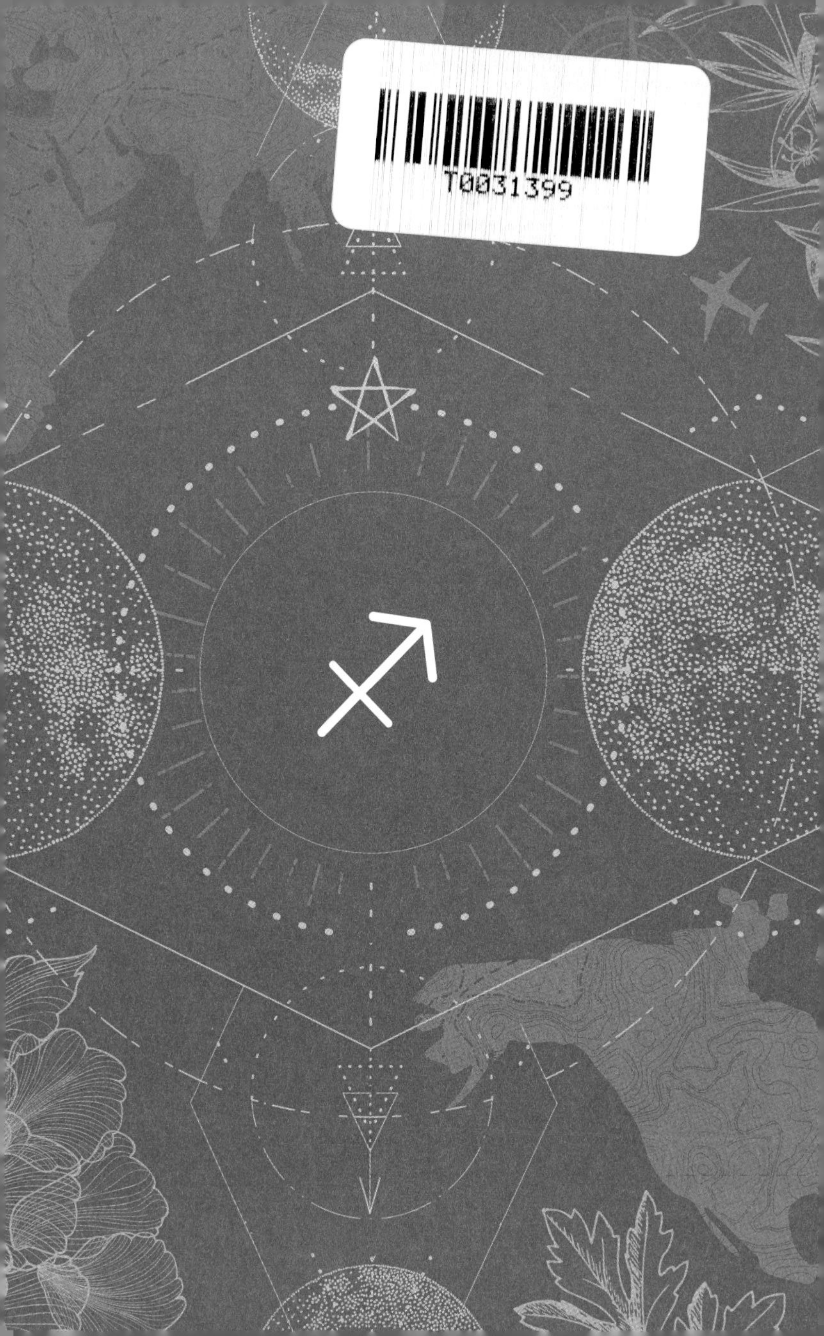
T0031399

SAGITTARIUS
WITCH

About the Authors

Ivo Dominguez, Jr. (Georgetown, DE) has been active in the magickal community since 1978. He is one of the founders of Keepers of the Holly Chalice, the first Assembly of the Sacred Wheel coven. He currently serves as one of the Elders in the Assembly. Ivo is the author of several books, including *The Four Elements of the Wise* and *Practical Astrology for Witches and Pagans*. In his mundane life, he has been a computer programmer, the executive director of an AIDS/HIV service organization, a bookstore owner, and many other things. Visit him at www.ivodominguezjr.com.

About the Authors

Enfys J. Book (they/them) is the author of the Gold COVR award-winning *Queer Qabala: Nonbinary, Genderfluid, Omnisexual Mysticism & Magick* (Llewellyn, 2022). They are a nonbinary, bisexual clergy member within the Assembly of the Sacred Wheel tradition, and the High Priest of the Fellowship of the Ancient White Stag coven near Washington, DC. They are also the creator of majorarqueerna.com, a website devoted to queer magickal practice, and they host a podcast called *4 Quick Q's: Book Talk with Enfys* where they interview Pagan authors using questions determined by a roll of the dice.

UNLOCK THE MAGIC OF YOUR SUN SIGN

SAGITTARIUS WITCH

IVO DOMINGUEZ, JR.
ENFYS J. BOOK

Llewellyn Publications
Woodbury, Minnesota

First Edition
First Printing, 2024

Art direction and cover design by Shira Atakpu
Book design by Christine Ha
Interior art by the Llewellyn Art Department
Tarot Original 1909 Deck © 2021 with art created by Pamela Colman Smith and Arthur Edward Waite. Used with permission of LoScarabeo.
The Sagittarius Correspondences appendix is excerpted with permission from *Llewellyn's Complete Book of Correspondences: A Comprehensive & Cross-Referenced Resource for Pagans & Wiccans* © 2013 by Sandra Kynes.
Photography is used for illustrative purposes only. The persons depicted may not endorse or represent the book's subject.

Library of Congress Cataloging-in-Publication Data
Names: Domínguez, Ivo, Jr., author. | Book, Enfys J., author.
Title: Sagittarius witch : unlock the magic of your sun sign the power of the arrow in flight / Ivo Dominguez, Jr. & Enfys J. Book.
Description: First edition. | Woodbury, MN : Llewellyn Worldwide ltd, 2024. | Series: The witch's sun sign series ; 9 | Includes bibliographical references.
Identifiers: LCCN 2023058960 (print) | LCCN 2023058961 (ebook) | ISBN 9780738772882 | ISBN 9780738772967 (ebook)
Subjects: LCSH: Sagittarius (Astrology) | Witchcraft. | Magic.
Classification: LCC BF1727.6 .D66 2024 (print) | LCC BF1727.6 (ebook) | DDC 133.5/274—dc23/eng/20240129
LC record available at https://lccn.loc.gov/2023058960
LC ebook record available at https://lccn.loc.gov/2023058961

Llewellyn Publications
A Division of Llewellyn Worldwide Ltd.
2143 Wooddale Drive
Woodbury, MN 55125-2989
www.llewellyn.com
Printed in the United States of America

Other Books by Ivo Dominguez, Jr.

The Four Elements of the Wise

Keys to Perception: A Practical Guide to Psychic Development

Practical Astrology for Witches and Pagans

Casting Sacred Space

Spirit Speak

Other Books by Enfys J. Book

Queer Qabala

Other Books in The Witch's Sun Sign Series

Aries Witch

Taurus Witch

Gemini Witch

Cancer Witch

Leo Witch

Virgo Witch

Libra Witch

Scorpio Witch

Capricorn Witch

Aquarius Witch

Pisces Witch

Disclaimer

CONTENTS

• SPELLS, RECIPES, AND PRACTICES •

INTRODUCTION

Ivo Dominguez, Jr.

This is the ninth book in the Witch's Sun Sign series. There are twelve volumes in this series with a book for every Sun sign, but with a special focus on witchcraft. This series explores and honors the gifts, perspectives, and joys of being a witch through the perspective of their Sun sign. Each book has information on how your sign affects your magick and life experiences with insights provided by witches of your Sun sign, as well as spells, rituals, and practices to enrich your witchcraft. This series is geared toward helping witches grow, develop, and integrate the power of their Sun sign into all their practices. Each book in the series has ten writers, so there are many takes on the meaning of being a witch of a particular sign. All the books in the Witch's Sun Sign series are a sampler of possibilities, with pieces that are deep, fun, practical, healing, instructive, revealing, and authentic.

Welcome to the Sagittarius Witch

I'm Ivo Dominguez, Jr., and I've been a witch and an astrologer for over forty years. In this book, and in the whole series, I've written the chapters focused on astrological information and collaborated with the other writers. For the sake of transparency, I am a Sagittarius, as are all but two of the writers for the book.[1] The chapters focused on the lived experience of being a Sagittarius witch were written by my coauthor, Enfys J. Book (they/them), the author of *Queer Qabala: Nonbinary, Genderfluid, Omnisexual Mysticism & Magick*. They are also a singer and songwriter, run a coven in the DC area, and work to break down limiting binaries in magickal theory and practice. The spells and shorter pieces written for this book come from a diverse group of strong Sagittarius witches. Their practices will give you a deeper understanding of yourself as a Sagittarius and as a witch. With the information, insights, and methods offered here, your Sagittarius nature and your witchcraft will be better united. The work of becoming fully yourself entails finding, refining, and merging all the parts that make up your life and identity. This all sounds very serious, but the content of this book will run from lighthearted to profound to do justice to the topic. Moreover, this book has practical suggestions on using the power of your Sun

1. The exceptions are two Scorpios: Dawn Aurora Hunt, who contributes a recipe for each sign in the series; and Sandra Kynes, whose correspondences are listed in the appendix.

sign to improve your craft as a witch. There are many books on Sagittarius or astrology or witchcraft; this book is about wholeheartedly being a Sagittarius witch.

There is a vast amount of material available in books, blogs, memes, and videos targeted at Sagittarius. The content presented in these ranges from serious to snarky, and a fair amount of it is less than accurate or useful. After reading this book, you will be better equipped to tell which of these you can take to heart and use, and which are fine for a laugh but not much more. There is a good chance you will be flipping back to reread some chapters to get a better understanding of some of the points being made. This book is meant to be read more than once, and some parts of it may become reference material you will use for years. Consider keeping a folder, digital or paper, for your notes and ideas on being a Sagittarius witch.

What You Will Need

Knowing your Sun sign is enough to get quite a bit out of this book. However, to use all the material in this book, you will need your birth chart to verify your Moon sign and rising sign. In addition to your birth date, you will need the location and the time of your birth as exactly as possible. If you don't know your birth time, try to get a copy of your birth certificate (though not all birth certificates list times). If it is reasonable and you feel comfortable, you can ask family members for information. They may remember an exact time, but even narrowing it down to a range of hours will be useful. There is a solution to not having your exact birth time. Since it takes moments to create birth charts using software, you can run birth charts that are thirty minutes apart over the span of hours that contains your possible birth times. By reading the chapters that describe the characteristics of Moon signs and rising signs, you can reduce the pile of possible charts to a few contenders. Read the descriptions and find the chart whose combination of Moon sign and rising sign rings true to you. There are more refined techniques a professional astrologer can use to get closer to a chart that is more accurate. However, knowing your Sun sign, Moon sign, and rising sign is all you need for this book. There are numerous websites that offer free basic birth charts you can view online. For a fee, more detailed charts are available on these sites.

You may want to have an astrological wall calendar or an astrological day planner to keep track of the sign and phase of the Moon. You will want to keep track of what your ruling planet, Jupiter, is doing. Over time as your knowledge grows, you'll probably start looking at where all the planets are, what aspects they are making, and when they are retrograde or direct. You could do this all on an app or a website, but it is often easier to flip through a calendar or planner to see what is going on. Flipping forward and back through the weeks and months ahead can give you a better sense of how to prepare for upcoming celestial influences. Moreover, the calendars and planner contain basic background information about astrology and are a great start for studying astrology.

You're a Sagittarius and So Much More

Every person is unique, complex, and a mixture of traits that can clash, complement, compete, or collaborate with each other. This book focuses on your Sagittarius Sun sign and provides starting points for understanding your Moon sign and rising sign. It cannot answer all your questions or be a perfect fit because of all the other parts that make you an individual. However, you will find more than enough to enrich and deepen your witchcraft as a Sagittarius. There will also be descriptions you won't agree with or you think do not portray you. In some instances, you will be correct, and in other cases, you may come around to acknowledging that the information does apply to you. Astrology can be used for magick, divination, personal development, and more. No matter the purpose, your understanding of astrology will change over time as your life unfolds and your experience and self-knowledge broaden. You will probably return to this book several times as you find opportunities to use more of the insights and methods.

This may seem like strange advice to find in a book for the Sagittarius witch, but remember that you are more than a Sagittarius witch. In the process of claiming the identity of being a witch, it is common to want to have a clear and firm definition of who you are. Sometimes this means overidentifying with a category, such as fire witch, herb witch, crystal witch, kitchen witch, and so on. It is useful to become aware of the affinities you have so long as you do not limit and bind yourself to being less than you are. The best use for this book is to uncover all the Sagittarius parts of you so you can integrate them well. The finest witches I know have well-developed specialties but also are well rounded in their knowledge and practices.

Onward!

With all that said, the Sun is the starting point for your power and your journey as a witch. The first chapter is about the profound influence your Sun sign has, so don't skip through the table of contents; please start at the beginning. After that, Enfys will dive into magick and practices that come naturally to Sagittarius witches. I'll be walking you through the benefits of picking the right times, places, and things to energize your Sagittarius magick. Enfys will also share a couple of real-life personal stories on how to manage the busy lives that Sagittarians choose, as well as advice on the best ways to protect yourself spiritually and set good boundaries when you really need to. I'll introduce you to how your Moon sign and your rising sign shape your witchcraft. Enfys offers great stories about how their Sagittarius nature comes forward in their life as a witch, and then gives suggestions on self-care and self-awareness. I'll share a full ritual with you to call on the spirit of your sign. Lastly, Enfys offers their wisdom on how to become a better Sagittarius witch. Throughout the whole book, you'll find tables of correspondences, spells, recipes, practices, and other treasures to add to your practices.

HOW YOUR SUN POWERS YOUR MAGICK

Ivo Dominguez, Jr.

The first bit of astrology people generally learn is their Sun sign. Some enthusiastically embrace the meaning of their Sun sign and apply it to everything in their life. They feel their Sun is shining and all is well in the world. Then at some point, they'll encounter someone who will, with a bit of disdain, enlighten them on the limits of Sun sign astrology. They feel their Sun isn't enough, and they scramble to catch up. What comes next is usually the discovery that they have a Moon sign, a rising sign, and all the rest of the planets in an assortment of signs. Making sense of all this additional information is daunting as it requires quite a bit of learning and/or an astrologer to guide you through the process. Wherever you are on this journey into the world of astrology, at some point you will circle back around and rediscover that the Sun is still in the center.

The Sun in your birth chart shows where life and spirit came into the world to form you. It is the keeper of your spark of spirit and the wellspring of your power. Your Sun is in Sagittarius, so that is the flavor, the color, the type of energy that is at your core. You are your whole birth chart, but it is your Sagittarius Sun that provides the vital force that moves throughout all parts of your life. When you work in harmony and alignment with your Sun, you have access to more life and the capacity to live it better. This is true for all people, but this advice takes on a special meaning for those who are witches. The root of a witch's magick power is revealed by their Sun sign. You can draw on many kinds of energy, but the type of energy you attract with greatest ease is Sagittarius. The more awareness and intention you apply to connecting with and acting as a conduit for that Sagittarius Sun, the more effective you will be as a witch.

The more you learn about the meaning of a Sagittarius Sun, the easier it will be to find ways to make that connection. To be effective in magick, divination, and other categories of workings, it is vital to understand yourself—your motivations, drives, attractions, etc.—so you can refine your intentions, questions, and desired outcomes.

Understanding your Sun sign is an important step in that process. One of the goals shared by both witchcraft and astrology is to affirm and to integrate the totality of your nature to live your best life. The glyph for the Sun in astrology is a dot with a circle around it. Your Sagittarius Sun is the dot and the circle, your center, and your circumference. It is your beginning and your journey. It is also the core of your personal Wheel of the Year, the seasons of your life that repeat, have resonances, but are never the same.

How Sagittarius Are You?

The Sun is the hub around which the planets circle. Its gravity pulls the planets to keep them in their courses and bends space-time to create the place we call our solar system. The Sun in your birth chart tugs on every other part of your chart in a similar way. Everything is both bound and free, affected but seeking its own direction. When people encounter descriptions of Sagittarius traits, they will often begin to make a list of which things apply to them and which don't. Some will say they are the epitome of Sagittarius traits, others will claim that they are barely Sagittarius, and many will be somewhere in between. Evaluating how closely or not you align with the traditional characteristics of a Sagittarius is not a particularly useful approach to understanding your sign. If you are a Sagittarius, you have all the Sagittarius traits somewhere within you. What varies from person to person is the expression of those traits. Some traits express fully in a classic form, others are blocked from expressing or are modified, and sometimes there is a reaction to behave as the opposite of what is expected. As a Sagittarius, and especially as a witch, you have the capacity to activate dormant traits, to shape functioning traits, and to tone down overactive traits.

The characteristics and traits of signs are tendencies, drives, and affinities. Gravity encourages a ball to roll down a hill. A plant's leaves will grow in the direction of sunlight. The warmth of a fire will draw people together on a cold night. A flavor you enjoy will entice you to take another bite of your food. Your Sagittarius Sun urges you to be and to act like a Sagittarius. That said, you also have free will and volition to make other choices. Moreover, the rest of your birth chart and the ever-changing celestial influences are also shaping your options, moods, and drives. The more you become aware of the traits and behaviors that come with being a Sagittarius, the easier it will be to choose how you express them. Most people want to have the freedom to make their own choices, but for a Sagittarius, it is essential.

As a witch, you have additional tools to work with the Sagittarius energy. You can choose when to access and how you shape the qualities of Sagittarius as they come forth in your life. You can summon the energy of Sagittarius, name the traits you desire, and manifest them. You can also banish or neutralize or ground what you don't need. You can find where your Sagittarius energy short-circuits, where it glitches, and unblock it. You can examine your uncomfortable feelings and your less-than-perfect behaviors to seek the shadowed places within so you can heal or integrate them. Sagittarius is also a spirit and a current of collective consciousness that is vast in size—a group mind and archetype. Sagittarius is not limited to humanity; it engages with plants, animals, minerals, and all the physical and nonphysical beings of the Earth and all its associated realms. As a witch, you can call upon and work with the spiritual entity that is Sagittarius. You can live your life as a ritual. The motion of your life can be a dance to the tune and rhythm of the heavens.

The Sagittarius Glyph

The glyph for Sagittarius looks like a simplified arrow. There is a long line forming the shaft, two short lines angled off the end to form a point, and a short line cutting across the shaft that can be seen as either the string of the bow or the fletching of the feathers. The long line and point indicate energy and intention in motion. A Sagittarian's will and spirit is focused on picking the target and the trajectory. This is also soul joining with spirit at the point. The line across the back of the shaft is a crossroads. This is a crossroads that connects planes of reality and connects frames of reference, for it is the context that gives rise to the impetus to seek and to reach the next experience. This intersection is also the cross of matter, the joining of the elements that brings creation and evolution. It is in bringing together the lessons from the crossroads that a Sagittarius gives power and purpose to the flight of their arrow, the arc of their life. The glyphs for the other fire signs center on how the signs are shaped by their fire. The glyph for Sagittarius is centered on how their kind of fire is applied to the world. The arrow, a *sagitta,* is an implement, and *Sagittarius* means "archer," the one who uses it.

Let's zoom out from just the arrow of the glyph and see the whole centaur that is Sagittarius. There is the horse, the human, and the bow and arrow. The legs are the four elements of the world, and the horse represents your primal self. The human represents your soul, your intellect, and your heart. The bow and arrow represent your divine spark, your higher Self, and your journey. When a Sagittarius brings the three into unity, they are their best selves. When you are whole, you know where to aim your efforts and why. As you evolve, you realize that you are shooting for the stars or the horizon. In either case, it is a joy because growth never ends, and you will always have more to explore.

By meditating on the glyph, you will develop a deeper understanding of what it is to be a Sagittarius. You may also come up with your own personal gnosis or story about the glyph that can be a key that is uniquely yours. The glyph for Sagittarius can be used in a similar fashion to the scribing of an invoking pentacle that is used to open the gates to the elemental realms. However, instead of the elemental realms, this glyph opens the way to the realm of mind and spirit that is the source of Sagittarius. To make this glyph work, you need to deeply ingrain the feeling of scribing this glyph. Spend some time doodling the glyph on paper. Try drawing the glyph on your palm with a finger for several repetitions as that adds several layers of sensation and memory patterns.

Whenever you need access to more of your magickal energy, scribe the Sagittarius glyph in your mind, on your hand, in the air—however you can. Then pull and channel and feel your center fill with whatever you need. It takes very little time to open this connection using the glyph. Consider making this one of the practices you use to get ready to do divination, spell work, ritual, or just to start your day.

Sagittarius Patterns

This is a short list of patterns, guidelines, and predilections for Sagittarius Sun people to get you started. If you keep a book of shadows, or a journal, or files on a digital device to record your thoughts and insights on magickal work, you may wish to create your own list to expand upon these. The process of observing, summarizing, and writing down your own ideas in a list is a great way to learn about your sign.

- Sagittarians tend be hopeful, not because the world is good or just, but because they will make it so someday. This Sun sign knows that it will rise again.
- You learn by experience and learn the most when you pay attention to the meaning of your mistakes.
- You are attracted to cultures, religions, philosophies, and people that are different from your own. This springs from the liberation that comes of knowing the world from other perspectives.

- If there is a new theory, a paradigm, freshly coined words, or anything else that expands your mind and pushes back the boundaries, you want to know about it.
- You are always looking for the next shiny thing that will consume all your time and focus that you will honestly declare is your new calling, until it is not. The good news is that it is not time wasted; it is skills and knowledge gained.
- You can be diplomatic and careful with your words, but it is just as likely that truth bombs will fall out of your mouth. When you realize that harm has been done, you do your best to make it right. However, try not to say, "Sorry I hurt you by telling you the truth."
- It is easy to get in touch with your inner child, but also your inner teenager, toddler, old coot, uptight adult, and so on. You have access to the full spectrum of selves you will be in your life. The trick is to call forth with the healthiest and wisest of all your versions.

- You love having fun and encouraging others to enjoy life. You have a gift for opening the circle to include new people.
- You are so passionate about your beliefs, your principles, even the trivia you know that you can stubbornly cling to statements you have begun to doubt. Sagittarians hate to be wrong, but hypocrisy is worse, so you yield to the truth in the end.
- Rogues and rangers, students and scholars, or philosophers and pontiffs are among the roles and characters that Sagittarians easily adopt.
- Sagittarians try to squeeze several lives' worth of experience into one lifetime. Your time on the planet is not long enough to do all you desire. This feeling can have the side effect of causing procrastination or moving on before finishing a task completely. Remind yourself of the sacredness of your will and word.

- You're always looking for the big picture, how it all works, and what it means in the long run. You do this because you want your choices and actions to be in alignment with higher principles, ethics, and your understanding of the spiritual realms. Matters of honor or principles are always high stakes for you.
- Jupiter is your ruling planet, so more always seems better to you. You are drawn to excess and overindulgence, so cultivate moderation.
- You were built for questing. These quests may involve travel in the physical world, or in the realm of ideas, or in the imaginal realms of politics, philosophy, or religion. If you are not on a quest, a mission, you'll get bored. Sagittarians dread boredom more than monsters and falling into a black hole.
- You are mutable fire, so your passions and anger can flare up quickly and forcefully, and then dwindle back quickly to a tidy little fire. This is why others are still upset when you've already moved on and think of an incident as being in the past.

Autonomy, freedom, personal sovereignty, and all related concepts connected to the power to make your own choices and to go your own way are like food and water to a Sagittarian. Without them, you weaken and die.

Mutable Fire

The four elements come in sets of three that repeat. The modalities known as cardinal, fixed, and mutable are three different flavors or styles of manifestation for the elements. The twelvefold pattern that is the backbone of astrology comes from the twelve combinations produced from four elements times three modalities. As you go around the wheel of the zodiac, the order of the elements is always fire, earth, air, then water, while the modalities are always in the order of cardinal, fixed, then mutable. Each season begins in the cardinal modality, reaches its peak in the fixed modality, and transforms to the next season in the mutable modality. The cardinal modality is the energy of creation bursting forth, coming into being, and spreading throughout the world. The fixed modality is the harmonization of energy so that it becomes and remains fully itself and is preserved. *Fixed* does not mean static or passive; it is the work of maintaining creation. The mutable modality is the energy of flux that is flexibility, transformation, death, and rebirth.

Sagittarius is the ninth sign in the zodiac, so it is fire of the mutable modality. This is why a Sagittarius witch can call upon deep reserves of life force and has the ability to easily shape and direct their magick. Although as a Sagittarius witch you can call upon fire in all its forms, it is easiest to draw upon mutable fire.

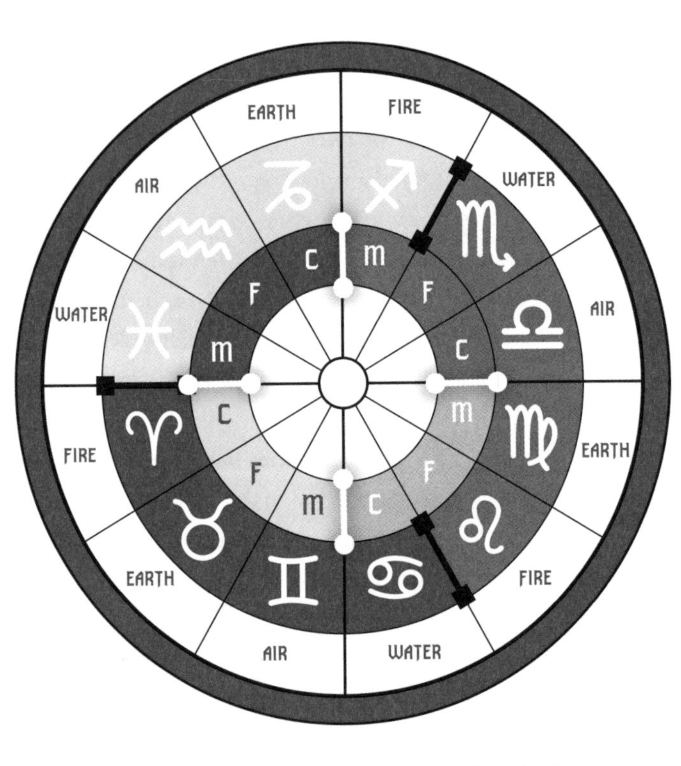

The elements and modalities on the wheel

Jupiter, Your Ruling Planet

♃

Your Sun sign determines the source and the type of energy you have in your core. The ruling planet for a sign reveals your go-to moves and your intuitive or habitual responses for expressing that energy. Your ruling planet provides a curated set of prebuilt responses and custom-tailored stances for you to use in day-to-day life. Jupiter is the ruling planet for Sagittarius. This may bring to mind the Greek Zeus or the Roman Jove, the chiefs of their pantheons. However, how the planet Jupiter influences Sagittarius is more complicated than being a sky father god. Jupiter's vantage point gives a broad view that allows it to understand how things fit together and how they interact. Seeing more possibilities results in Jupiter being the planet of growth, hope, grace, and law giving. Jupiter is also mentoring, teaching, and preaching. Jupiter is the desire for wisdom. This in turn gives a strong desire to explore as much as possible. The influence of Jupiter makes Sagittarius seek joy through unending learning and the sharing of what they have found.

Sagittarius witches are more strongly affected by whatever Jupiter is doing in the heavens. It is useful to keep track of the aspects that Jupiter is making with other planets. You can get basic information on what aspects mean and when they are happening in astrological calendars and online resources. You will feel Jupiter retrogrades strongly, but you can find ways to make them useful periods to review and to rework plans. Sagittarius witches will notice that the impact of the Jupiter retrograde will start earlier and end a few days later than the listed duration. Also, when Jupiter in the heavens is in Sagittarius, you will feel an extra boost of energy. The first step to using the power of Jupiter is to pay attention to what it is doing, how you feel, and what is happening in your life.

Witches have the gift to shift their relationship with the powers they work with and the powers that influence them. As a Sagittarius witch, you are connected to the power of Jupiter. By paying close attention to how those energies affect you, it becomes possible to harness those energies to purposes *you* choose. Jupiter can be as great a source of energy for a Sagittarius witch as the element of fire. Although there is some overlap between the qualities and capacities assigned to Jupiter and fire, the differences are greater. Jupiter is generative and causes growth by choosing the right path or procedure. Fire is the medium that is life and drives growth. Jupiter has the power to encourage and to inspire. Fire is the energy that powers actions. Jupiter is laden with layers of meaning, connections, and abstractions. Jupiter creates systems to express, distribute, and enshrine the divine. Fire is the sacred essence itself that is the spark of creation. Over time, you can map out the overlapping regions and the differences between Jupiter and fire. Using both planetary and elemental resources can give you a much broader range and more finesse.

Sagittarius and the Zodiacal Wheel

The order of the signs in the zodiac can also be seen as a creation story where the run of the elements repeats three times. Sagittarius is in the last third of the zodiac, which is the third appearance of the four elements in the story of the universe. They are far from the start of creation; they are on the return journey to the source. Sagittarius wants to achieve the quest to return to the beginning. The fire of Sagittarius is the most nuanced of all the versions of the element of fire.

Although true for all witches, the Sagittarius witch needs to apply themselves to living in the physical world while remaining aware of their divine spark. When you can regularly connect with your divine Self, you are a change maker, and the people and projects that matter to you will flourish. This is the full expression of being in the last third of the zodiac. You can make progress in this quest through meditation and inner journeys, but that alone will not do. The Sagittarius witch develops by seeing, touching, questioning, practicing, and teaching. Although Sagittarians are sometimes stereotyped as opinionated and overly optimistic, it is more accurate to say that they speak with passion and trust their abilities. When a Sagittarius witch connects to the spiritual qualities of their fire, they become whole and an agent of the magick of the world.

The sign and planet rulers on the zodiac wheel

SAGITTARIUS CORRESPONDENCES

Power: To Understand

Keyword: Planning

Roles: Adventurer, Philosopher, Optimist

Ruling Planet: Jupiter ♃

Element: Mutable Fire 

Colors: Royal Blue, Navy Blue, Indigo

Shape: Square

Metal: Tin

Body Part Ruled: Hips and Thighs

Day of the Week: Thursday

Affirmation:

Let my fiery enthusiasm be tempered by kindness to self and others.

WITCHCRAFT THAT COMES NATURALLY TO A SAGITTARIUS

Enfys J. Book

Sagittarians are born curious and love to explore new things, so we're really able to do any type of witchcraft we develop a passion for. But there are certain types of magick that will be easier for us to pick up and excel at, thanks to our Sun sign.

Reality Maps and Frameworks for Understanding Life and the Universe

The classic archetypal symbol of Sagittarius is that of a centaur aiming a bow and arrow toward the heavens. Like that centaur, Sagittarians quest to touch divinity, and to know, understand, and be connected to all life, the universe, and the divine source of all. We are creatures who love thinking Big Thoughts and sharing with others what we've learned or what we're currently pondering. We're natural students, teachers, and philosophers. We love geeking out about our passions.

Even if we aren't subscribed to any particular form of spirituality or religion, Sagittarians have a deep yearning to understand the meaning of life and to connect with the numinous. As a result, we tend to be drawn to big-picture systems and philosophies that help us understand and explain how things fit together. For example, I got hooked on Hermetic Qabala from the moment I started studying it, because it's a framework for understanding personal growth, how the universe works, and our relationship with divinity. Having the visual key of the Tree of Life glyph to help understand magick, the process of manifestation, and the different levels of consciousness inspired me in a huge way, and I geeked out on it so hard that I ended up writing a book on the subject, and have another book about it in process as I write this.

Qabala is just one example of what Christopher Penczak and other occultists call "reality maps."[2] There are many other maps that Sagittarians may be drawn to, which vary by spiritual tradition, like the Norse world tree Yggdrasil, for example. Beyond "reality maps," we also groove on detailed

2. Christopher Penczak, *The Temple of High Witchcraft* (Woodbury, MN: Llewellyn, 2007), 69.

systems like alchemy, astrology, numerology, chakras, sacred geometry, or any number of occult subjects. We love to learn theories and then apply them practically—or break them down and rebuild them into something better. We love taking something abstract and applying it in a way that makes sense in day-to-day life and our magickal practice. This is why we can be excellent teachers and writers on the occult, witchcraft, and polytheism; we absorb and transmute information into something others can understand and apply.

Spirit Work

Sagittarians are also natural spirit workers, because we love to explore, travel, and learn, and that includes traveling to the other realms through pathworking and astral journeying. Our mutable nature lends itself well to shape-shifting and communicating with beings very different from ourselves. Those communication skills also help us call in and banish spirits. Similarly, divine possession in its many forms tends to be right in the Sagittarian wheelhouse, because we can shift and mold our energy with ease.

A word of caution here: though spirit work may be an area where you find a natural talent, when you are starting out, it's important to approach this sort of work with lots of open-mindedness and humility, particularly if you are using spirit work to guide others. Our optimism and strongly opinionated nature (let's face it, we can be pretty arrogant sometimes) can lead to us mistaking our own views for those of the spirits we're communicating with. If you find yourself agreeing with everything you encounter, and not finding many surprises along the way, take a step back and examine your practice to find places where you could open your mind and listen more closely. It's helpful to have mentors to help you distinguish and validate the messages you're receiving.

Catalyzing Change and Sparking Courage

One of the many properties of elemental fire is that it can catalyze change. Sagittarians are especially well suited toward this kind of magick, because the concept of mutability is built into our Sun sign and because a lot of us intentionally live very dynamic lives, regularly chasing new adventures, fields of study, and career paths. I find that I'm rarely bored or deeply dissatisfied in my life, because I tend to be proactive about changing situations that aren't tenable, and the changes I make tend to stick. I also have a tendency to catalyze big changes in other people's lives, often without being consciously aware of that influence. If you have a friend who needs to get out of a rut and asks for your aid, you are well positioned to help give their situation a magickal nudge.

A Spell for Courage

Enfys J. Book

Life throws a lot of scary stuff at us that may, at times, test our resilience. Fortunately, fire can fuel our ability to push through a rough time. If you're facing a difficult situation and need to bolster your courage, this spell will help. For extra power, do this working on a full Moon. Be sure to cleanse the stone, in whatever manner befits your practice, before using it in this ritual.

You will need:

- A reddish stone (e.g., red jasper)
- A small red candle—either a tealight or a chime candle
- A candleholder
- A lighter or match
- A mirror

Instructions:

Breathe deeply. Ground and center yourself (see the Simple Cleansing, Grounding, Centering, and Shielding Meditation on page 69 if you're unsure how to do this).

Put the candle in the candleholder. While lighting the candle, say, "I call upon my guides and guardians to lend me courage."

If you work with specific spirits or deities, invoke them by name. Tell them, out loud, about the situation and where your confidence is faltering.

Breathe deeply and listen for a while. Your guides may have advice for you.

Hold up the stone with your dominant hand and say, "I ask for aid to enchant this stone with extra courage, so I can call upon it when I need to."

Breathe deeply, and on your exhale, visualize yourself being courageous, feel that courage in your bones, and push that image and that energy into the stone. Repeat this as many times as you feel is needed, until the stone is nice and buzzy and feels strong in your hand.

Now, hold the stone in your nondominant hand, gaze into your eyes in the mirror, and say five times, with conviction, "I can do this."

Thank your guides for their assistance. Breathe deeply, and ground and center yourself once more.

Each day, when you get up in the morning, hold the stone in your nondominant hand, gaze into your eyes in a mirror, and say "I can do this" five times. Draw courageous energy from the stone.

Carry the stone with you when you need an extra boost of courage. Recharge the stone at the full Moon by repeating this working.

Sex Magic

Sexual energy is a power source that can be used in a sacred, ritual context to release emotional and spiritual blocks, heal, and manifest your desires. Fire signs like us have the potential to be *fantastic* at sex magick (and, *ahem*, sex) if that's something we want to try. Whether by ourselves or with a partner or partners, we can channel the sexual fires within into some truly astounding and powerful magickal work. The next time you are doing a working that needs a huge energetic boost, sex magick may be a great fuel source for it.

Sex magick is great! But unfortunately, sex magick can also be easily used unethically to manipulate people, particularly newbie witches, so I'm going to take a quick couple of paragraphs to cover that. A full course in sex magick how-tos and ethics is beyond the scope of this little section of a chapter, but for an introductory taste, I recommend the chapter "Safer Sex Magic for Beginners (and Experts)" found in Misha Magdalene's book *Outside the Charmed Circle: Exploring Gender & Sexuality in Magical Practice*. There are also several books specifically about sex magick that deal with this subject more comprehensively, though I don't have any specific recommendations as of the time I'm writing this.

On with the caveats: physical, sexual intimacy makes us particularly emotionally and physically vulnerable, so extra care is needed when approaching this kind of magick. If you're doing sex magick with others, don't do it spur-of-the-moment.

Think about what you want to do and why, and discuss it with those with whom you want to do it *ahead of time*. (Like, *way* ahead of time. When you're in a *conversation* headspace rather than a *sexy* headspace.) Make sure to be transparent about what you plan to do, talk it through, and establish trust *first*. Consider all concerns you and your partner(s) may have before any magickal sexytimes. Ask questions. Don't make assumptions about what you or they want. Don't pressure anyone to participate. Discuss safety precautions, both magickal and mundane (side note: magick is no substitute for a condom or birth control, and don't let anyone tell you otherwise). Be clear that you can stop anytime if someone is not comfortable with what's happening. Informed consent is *required*, and it is deeply unfair and unethical to suddenly spring a magickal working on someone you're in the middle of having sex with.

And never, ever make promises about what sex magick can accomplish, or portray it as the only way to achieve or awaken something magickally. Like far too many witches, I've had some bad experiences with unethical teachers trying to get me into bed with the promise of some grand personal evolution that could, supposedly, *only* be accomplished through sex, with them. (For the record, such claims are utter bullshit.) Unfortunately, people using sex magick in a predatory fashion are way too common.

All that said, if sex magick is something you want to explore, and you're working in a good ethical framework either on your own or with a consenting partner or partners, go for it.

Luck and Prosperity Magic

With Jupiter as the ruling planet of Sagittarius, luck and prosperity magick comes naturally to us as well. And who doesn't need more luck and prosperity? You can enhance the power of luck or prosperity spells by incorporating Jupiter's glyph (see page 23) somewhere in the working, or by timing it during Jupiter's day (Thursday) or during Jupiter's hour (search for planetary hours online or use a planetary hours app to find out when that will be; they change every day). Any one of these will help, but doing all three will add the most powerful bang for your magickal buck.

Note that luck and prosperity magick requires mundane actions to support them. Luck and prosperity spells help move energies in your favor, but you can't count on them to flip a situation all on their own. For example, if you don't send out resumes, it's unlikely you'll get a job offer, no matter how good a spell you cast. If you half-ass your studying, it's unlikely you'll get a good grade, even with an awesome good luck charm. Magick by itself is going to have a hard time manifesting your desires all on its own, so try to do everything in your power in the mundane world to align a situation in your favor, then use luck or prosperity spells to nudge things over the finish line.

Fire-Related Magic

Any magick involving fire is a no-brainer for us. Candle magick, making magickal incense, scrying into fire, sending intentions and releasing things by burning paper, dancing around a fire to build energy for a working... all of that plays to our strengths as fiery beings, and can help bolster our own fiery energy. Consider incorporating fire into your regular magickal practice, even if it's something as simple as lighting a stick of incense each day. Regularly draw the energy from fire into yourself, setting an intention to rekindle your passion and joy for life and magickal work. Though our enthusiasm as magickal practitioners may feel limitless, we all get burned out sometimes (pun intended), and regularly working with fire energy to recharge can help you recover.

Working with Groups, and Creating and Leading Group Rituals

Our Sagittarian enthusiasm can be channeled into great, powerful work as a solo practitioner, because enthusiasm is excellent fuel for magick, and there's a seemingly endless wellspring of energy within us! But Sagittarians tend to work particularly well with other people, especially other Sagittarians and other fire signs. When we are at our best, we can use all our phenomenal Jupiter energy to be charismatic and inspirational group leaders, and contribute a lot of great ideas and energy to the groups we're part of.

Sagittarians have a flair for drama and we revel in rituals that stimulate multiple senses, which means we have a knack for creating and leading theatrical and immersive rituals. Think makeup, costumes, and music that help you and participants get into ritual headspace and connect on a deeper level. Appealing to multiple senses, which is sometimes referred to in magickal work as "smells and bells," can really help guide people toward powerful magickal outcomes. When you're writing a ritual, consider adding some additional visual, auditory, scent, tactile, or taste cues—even just describing them within a pathworking—to better immerse everyone in the work.

Healing

Have you heard of Chiron, the wounded healer centaur of classical Greek folklore? Our connection to centaurs, as well as our mutable nature, can make us exceptional healers as well. The mutable modality seeks balance, and health and healing are about *re*balancing someone's physical and subtle bodies so their systems work in harmony. Mutable energy is also resilient and adaptable to changing circumstances, shifting where it needs to shift and holding where it needs to hold. Being mutable helps us be flexible when we experience upheavals in our life or changes in our health. We pay attention to our own bodies and can tune in to our own needs, which then helps us apply that same connection to others. Our mutable nature can help others shift their energy to help bring their energetic and physical bodies back into balance.

The Sky's the Limit

Sagittarians have a lot of natural tendencies and gifts that help us excel at certain kinds of magick. If you don't see your strengths in this chapter, don't fear! This list is only meant to spark some inspiration, and it is not comprehensive. Sagittarians are full of passion and can direct that passion toward excelling in a wide variety of things, even things that may not seem a natural fit for a Sagittarius. Our mutable nature combined with our natural curiosity and boundless enthusiasm is a fantastic recipe for succeeding at anything we put our minds to.

MAGICAL CORRESPONDENCES

Enfys J. Book

Let's face it: certain types of magick are simply *your jam* as a Sagittarius. Some things just come more naturally to you. Your innate enthusiasm and seemingly boundless energy can be put to good use in any type of magick you set your mind to, but here are some ideas for types of spells, workings, and tools that align well with fiery Sagittarius energy.

Types of Spellcraft

- Candle magick
- Leading theatrical rituals
- Sex magick
- Healing magick
- Spirit work and shape-shifting
- Working with, calling in, and banishing spirits

Magical Tools

- Wand or athame, depending on your magickal tradition
- Sword or staff, depending on your magickal tradition
- Arrowheads
- Broomstick
- Your body (dancing, sacred movement, etc.)

Magical Goals and Spell Ideas

- Social justice magick
- Prosperity and luck magick
- Increasing courage, motivation, stamina, or endurance
- Helping change or bring resolution to a situation
- Uncovering truth
- Finding your life's purpose or divine will

TIMING, PLACES, AND THINGS

Ivo Dominguez, Jr.

You've probably encountered plenty of charts and lists in books and online cataloguing which things relate to your Sun sign and ruling planet. There are many gorgeously curated assortments of herbs, crystals, music playlists, fashions, sports, fictional characters, tarot cards, and more that are assigned to your Sun sign. These compilations of associations are more than a curiosity or for entertainment. Correspondences are like treasure maps to show you where to find the type and flavor of power you are seeking. Correspondences are flowcharts and diagrams that show the inner occult relationships between subtle energies and the physical world. Although there are many purposes for lists of correspondences, there are two that are especially valuable to becoming a better Sagittarius witch. The first is to contemplate the meaning of the correspondences, the ways in which they reveal meaningful details about your Sun sign and ruling planet, and how they connect to you. This will deepen your understanding of what it is to be a Sagittarius witch. The second is to use these items as points of connection to access energies and essences that support your witchcraft. This will expand the number of tools and resources at your disposal for all your efforts.

Each of the sections in this chapter will introduce you to a type of correlation with suggestions on how to identify and use it. These are just starting points, and you will find many more as you explore and learn more. As you broaden your knowledge, you may find yourself a little bit confused as you find that sources disagree on the correlations. These contradictions are generally not a matter of who is in error but a matter of perspective, cultural differences, and the intended uses for the correlations. Anything that exists in the physical world can be described as a mixture of all the elements, planets, and signs. You may be a Sagittarius, but depending on the rest of your chart, there may be strong concentrations of other signs and elements. For example, if you find that a particular herb is listed as associated with both Sagittarius and Gemini, it is because it contains both natures in abundance. In the cases of strong multiple correlations, it is important that you summon or tune in to the one you need.

Times

You always have access to your power as a Sagittarius witch, but there are times when the flow is stronger or more easily summoned. There are sophisticated astrological methods to select dates and times that are specific to your birth chart. Unless you want to learn quite a bit more astrology or hire someone to determine these for you, you can do quite well with simpler methods. Let's look at the cycles of the solar year, the lunar month, and the hours of day-night rotation. When the Sun is in Sagittarius, or the Moon is in Sagittarius, or it is approaching midnight, you are in the sweet spot for tuning in to the core of your power.

Sagittarius season is roughly November 22 to December 21, but check your astrological calendar to determine when it is for a specific year in your time zone. The amount of energy that is accessible is highest when the Sun is at the same degree of Sagittarius as it is in your birth chart. This peak will not always be on your birth date, but very close to it. Midway through Sagittarius season at the fifteenth degree is another peak for all Sagittarians. Take advantage of Sagittarius season for working magick and for recharging and storing up energy for the whole year.

The Moon moves through the twelve signs every lunar cycle and spends around two and half days in each sign.

When the Moon is in Sagittarius, you have access to more lunar power because the Moon in the heavens has a resonant link to the Sun in your birth chart. At some point during its time in Sagittarius, the Moon will be at the same degree as your Sun. For you, that will be the energy peak during the Moon's passage through Sagittarius that month. While the Moon is in Sagittarius, your psychism is stronger, as is your ability to manifest things. When the Moon is a waning crescent in any sign, you can draw upon its power more readily because it is resonant to your sign.

There are no holidays during Sagittarius season like an equinox, solstice, or cross-quarter day. However, the peak of Sagittarius season at the midpoint, the fifteenth degree, is a day of peak mutability and a liminal space for your magick. Look up when the Sun is in the fifteenth degree of Sagittarius for the current or future years using online resources or an ephemeris. Sagittarius is the ninth sign of the zodiac, and the zodiac is like a clock for the purpose of spell work. The peak of night that leads up to the witching hour of midnight corresponds to the power of Sagittarius. If you are detail focused, you might be wondering when the peak of night is. This varies with the time of year and with your location, but it is generally 10:00 p.m. to 12:00 a.m. Or you can use your intuition and feel your way to when peak night has begun, when the sky is dark with mystery. The powers that flow during this time are filled with eagerness, possibilities, and quests for you to experience. Plan on using the Sagittarius energy of the night for inspiration and to feed spells for optimism, making plans, understanding occult mysteries, and personal growth.

The effect of these special times can be joined in any combination. For example, you can choose to do work during the peak of night, or when the Moon is in Sagittarius, or the Sun is in Sagittarius, or the Moon is in Sagittarius during Sagittarius season. You can combine all three as well. Each of these time groupings will have a distinctive feeling. Experiment and use your instincts to discover how to use these in your work.

Places

There are activities, professions, phenomena, and behaviors that have an affinity, a resonant connection, to Sagittarius and its ruling planet, Jupiter. These activities occur in the locations that suit or facilitate their expressions. There is magick to be claimed from those places that is earmarked for Sagittarius or your ruling planet, Jupiter. Just like your birth chart, the world around you contains the influences of all the planets and signs, but in different proportions and arrangements. You can always draw upon Sagittarius or

Jupiter energy, though there are times when it is more abundant depending on astrological considerations. Places and spaces have energies that accumulate and can be tapped like a battery. Places contain the physical, emotional, and spiritual environments that are created by the actions of the material objects, plants, animals, and people occupying those spaces. Some of the interactions between these things can generate or concentrate the energies and patterns that can be used by Sagittarius witches.

If you look at traditional astrology books, you'll find listings of places assigned to Sagittarius and Jupiter that include locations such as these:

- Scenic vistas, majestic views, inspiring landscapes
- Temples, houses of worship, sacred sites
- Universities, schools of higher or specialized learning
- Rowdy and boisterous bars, parties, and dance halls
- Airports, seaports, and all places that coordinate travel

These are very clearly linked to the themes associated with Sagittarius and Jupiter. With a bit of brainstorming and free-associating, you'll find many other less obvious locations and situations where you can draw upon this power. For example, wherever philosophers, politicians, or theologians are expounding or debating can produce a current you can plug into. Oddly enough, comedians and humor are a source of power too. Any situation where you follow your head and heart to take your shot regardless of risk or engage in large-scale projects can become a source of power for a Sagittarius witch. All implements or actions related to daring activities that open new horizons and bring fresh experiences could also be sources for energy.

While you can certainly go to places that are identified as locations where Sagittarius and/or Jupiter energy is plentiful to do workings, you can find those energies in many other circumstances. Don't be limited by the idea that the places must be the ones that have a formalized link to Sagittarius. Be on the lookout for Sagittarius or Jupiter themes and activities wherever you may be. Remember that people thinking, feeling, or participating in activities connected to your sign and its ruling planet are raising power. If you can identify with it as resonating with your Sun sign or ruling planet, then you can call the power and put it to use. You complete the circuit to engage the flow with your visualization, intentions, and actions.

Plants

Sagittarius seeks higher knowledge, adventure, mind expansion, and fun, and its colors are royal blue and bright amethyst. Jupiter encourages hope, expansion, a good-humored nature, luck, and healing. Herbs, resins, oils, fruits, vegetables, woods, and flowers that strongly exhibit one or more of these qualities can be called upon to support your magick. Here are a few examples:

- Hyssop for lightening your spirit.
- Carnations for luck.
- Yellow dock to free you from unwanted ties.
- Chervil for releasing and cleansing harsh emotions.
- Star anise for higher consciousness.

Once you understand the rationale for making these assignments, the lists of correspondences will make more sense. Another thing to consider is that each part of a plant may resonate more strongly with a different element, planet, and sign. Red carnation shows its connection with Sagittarius and Jupiter with its ease of growth and the hopefulness it brings. However, red carnation is also an herb of Aries and Mars because of its red color, jagged petals, and the protection it offers. White carnations do not align with Aries, only the red ones. Which energy steps forward depends on your call and invitation. *Like calls to like* is a truism in witchcraft. When you use your Sagittarius nature to make a call, you are answered by the Sagittarius part of the plant.

Plant materials can take the form of incense, anointing oils, altar pieces, potions, washes, magickal implements, foods, flower arrangements, and so on. The mere presence of plant material that is linked to Sagittarius or Jupiter will be helpful to you. However, to gain the most benefit from plant energy, you need to actively engage with it. Push some of your energy into the plants and then pull on it to start the flow. Although much of the plant material you work with will be dried or preserved, it retains a connection to living members of their species. You may also want to reach out and try to commune with the spirit, the group soul, of the plants to request their assistance or guidance. This will awaken the power slumbering in the dried or preserved plant material. Spending time with living plants, whether they be houseplants, in your yard, or in a public garden, will strengthen your conversation with the green beings under Sagittarius's eye.

Crystals and Stones

Before digging into this topic, let's clear up some of the confusion around the birthstones for the signs of the zodiac. There are many varying lists for birthstones. Also be aware that some are related to the calendar month rather than the zodiacal signs. There are traditional lists, but the most commonly available lists for birthstones were created by jewelers to sell more jewelry. Also be cautious of the word *traditional* as some jewelers refer to the older lists compiled by jewelers as "traditional." The traditional lists created by magickal practitioners also diverge from each other because of cultural differences and the availability of different stones in the times and places the lists were created. If you have already formed a strong connection to a birthstone that you discover is not really connected to the energy of your sign, keep using it. Your connection is proof of its value to you in moving, holding, and shifting energy, whether or not it is specifically attuned to Sagittarius.

These are my preferred assignments of birthstones for the signs of the zodiac:

Aries	Bloodstone, Carnelian, Diamond
Taurus	Rose Quartz, Amber, Sapphire
Gemini	Agate, Tiger's Eyes, Citrine
Cancer	Moonstone, Pearl, Emerald
Leo	Heliodor, Peridot, Black Onyx
Virgo	Green Aventurine, Moss Agate, Zircon
Libra	Jade, Lapis Lazuli, Labradorite
Scorpio	Obsidian, Pale Beryl, Nuummite
Sagittarius	Turquoise, Blue Topaz, Iolite
Capricorn	Black Tourmaline, Howlite, Ruby
Aquarius	Amethyst, Sugilite, Garnet
Pisces	Ametrine, Smoky Quartz, Aquamarine

There are many other possibilities that work just as well, and I suggest you find what responds best for you as an individual. I've included all twelve signs in case you'd like to use the stones for your Moon sign or rising sign. Hands-on experimentation is the best approach, so I suggest visiting crystal or metaphysical shops and rock and mineral shows when possible. Here's some information on the three that I prefer for Sagittarius.

Turquoise

Turquoise helps you remember who you are, the whole truth of your being. For Sagittarians, this helps in the ongoing work of uniting the animal, human, and divine within themselves. It is also a stone that helps moderate overheated enthusiasm without putting it out. It will also add energy to ideas and insights that are just beginning to awaken. Turquoise helps even out the highs and lows of Sagittarian mutability. It is a bridging or linking gem that helps connect heaven and Earth, different planes of being, the consciousness of different species, and so on. As such, it is a stone for visions, communication, and soul travel.

Blue Topaz

Blue topaz amplifies the projection of thoughts and enhances communication in summoning and banishing beings. It also helps strengthen your wards and shields. It can be used to take apart spells and curses. In meditation, it helps stimulate the development of wisdom, self-control, and discernment. It opens both the third eye and the throat chakras. Blue topaz helps you see opportunities and lucky breaks so that you can put them to good use. It augments your self-confidence and helps you see long-term consequences to your actions. This gem also gives the gift of eloquence and makes it easier to do public speaking.

Iolite

Iolite helps you pick a direction and is a stone of pathfinding and navigation. This is true for physical, mental, or spiritual journeys. It also is a crystal for creativity as it helps you find your way through the notes in a composition, the plot in a story, the choice of colors in your art, and so on. Iolite helps improve memory and speeds recollection. It can be used to ease your way into more restful sleep. Iolite works with your body to help expel spiritual toxins and unwanted energies. Emotionally, this stone supports you when you must face errors that you've made so you may correct what you can.

Intuition and spiritual guidance play a part in the making of correlations and, in the case of traditional lore, the collective experience of many generations of practitioners. There is also reasoning behind how these assignments are made and understanding the process will help you choose well. Here are some examples of this reasoning:

 Crystals assigned to Sagittarius are often shades of blue or purple, often with mottled colors to show its mutability. Sodalite and chevron amethyst are good examples of these.

- Sagittarius's metal is tin, so crystals such as cassiterite and wood tin resonate with Sagittarius magicks.
- Crystals whose lore and uses are related to Sagittarius or Jupiter actions or topics (prosperity, luck, spiritual experiences, and healing) such as charoite, moldavite, and pietersite are recommended for Sagittarius.
- Crystals that are the opposite of the themes for Sagittarius provide a counterbalance to an excessive manifestation of Sagittarius traits. For example, obsidian is on lists of crystals for many other signs but is useful for Sagittarius because it encourages grounded thinking.
- Crystals suggested for Gemini, your opposite sign, are also useful to maintain your balance. Tiger's eye is a good example of this principle.

Working with Ritual Objects

A substantial number of traditions or schools of witchcraft use magickal tools that are consecrated to represent and hold the power of the elements. Oftentimes in these systems there is one primary tool for each of the elements and other tools that are alternatives to these or are mixtures of elements. There are many possible combinations and reasons for why the elements are assigned to different tools in different traditions and they all work within their own context. Find and follow what works best for you. Magickal tools and ritual objects are typically cleansed, consecrated, and charged to prepare them for use. In addition to following whatever procedure you may have for preparing your tools, add in a step to incorporate your energy and identity as a Sagittarius witch. This is especially productive for magickal tools and ritual objects that are connected to Earth or are used to store, direct, or focus power. By adding Sagittarius energy and patterning into the preparation of your tools, you will find it easier to raise, move, and shape energy with them in your workings.

There are many magickal tools and ritual objects that do not have any attachment to specific elements. The core of your life force and magickal power springs from your Sagittarius Sun. So, when you consciously join your awareness of your Sagittarius core with the power flowing through the tools or objects, it increases their effectiveness. Adding your earthy energy does not make it an earth tool, it makes it a Sagittarius tool tuned to you. Develop the habit of using the name *Sagittarius* as a word of power, the glyph for Sagittarius for summoning power, and the greens and earthy neutral tones of Sagittarius to visualize its flow. Whether it be a pendulum, a wand, a crystal, or a chalice, your Sagittarius energy will be quick to rise and answer your call.

A Charging Practice

When you consciously use your Sagittarius witch energy to send power into tools, it tunes them more closely to your aura. Here's a quick method for imbuing any tool with your Sagittarius energy.

1. Place the tool in front of you on a table or altar.
2. Take a breath in, imagining that you are breathing in crimson or purple energy, and then say "Sagittarius" as you exhale. Repeat this three times.
3. Place your hands on your thighs, the part of the body ruled by Sagittarius, and draw in some energy. Lift your hands to chest level with palms facing each other. Touch your fingertips to form the shape of an arrowhead pointed away from you. Then bring both hands in close to your chest and cross them at your wrists to form an X. You have formed the glyph of Sagittarius.
4. Now, using a finger, trace the glyph of Sagittarius over or on the tool you are

charging. Repeat this several times and imagine the glyph being absorbed by the tool.

5. Pick up the tool, take in a breath while imagining royal blue energy, then blow that charged breath over the tool.
6. Say "Blessed be!" and proceed with using the tool or putting it away.

Hopefully this charging practice will inspire you and encourage you to experiment. Use the name *Sagittarius* as a word of power, the glyph for Sagittarius for summoning power, and the rich blue or amethyst colors of Sagittarius to visualize its flow whenever you can. Feel free to use these spontaneously in all your workings. Whether it be a pendulum, a wand, a crystal, a chalice, a ritual robe, or anything else that catches your imagination, these simple methods can have a large impact. The Sagittarius energy you imprint into objects will be quick to rise and answer your call.

HERBAL CORRESPONDENCES

These plant materials all have a special connection to your energy as a Sagittarius witch. There are many more, but these are a good starting point.

Herbs

Cedar	for protection and abundance
Juniper Berries	clarifies thoughts and speeds healing
Vervain	for taking the right action

Flowers

Borage	for courage and calm
Feverfew	heals magickal attacks and elfshot
Gladiolus	supports integrity and perserverance

Incense and Fragrances

Copal Oro	purifies and raises energy
Red Sandalwood	for opening the way and devotional work
Nutmeg	for psychism and justice spells

Cleansing and Shielding

Enfys J. Book

As a Sagittarius witch who tends to unconsciously soak up the energies around me, learning how to ground, center, cleanse, and shield as part of my daily practice has been life-changing. I think at least half my ambient anxiety in my youth and young adulthood was the result of not knowing how to move or manage my energy. These days, I ground, center, cleanse, and shield daily, and I notice a difference in how much better I feel when I do. I strongly recommend grounding and centering before and after any magickal work, and I recommend including at least grounding and shielding into your daily magickal practice.

If you're new to these concepts, don't stress: I'm going to explain what they are and how to do them in more detail. Let's start with some definitions, because *grounding, centering, cleansing,* and *shielding* all mean different things in different contexts, and they're terms that get thrown around a lot within witchy circles.

Grounding: Connecting with the Earth to both release excess energy from your body and energetic fields and draw up energy you need.

Centering: Moving your center of consciousness, with intent, to a place of balance within your body to enhance your clarity and focus.

Cleansing: Removing unwanted energy or connections from your energetic bodies, or from a space or object.

Shielding: Protecting your space and personal energetic fields from attack or interference. Shielding your space and yourself will make daily cleansing easier, because you'll be preventing the formation of unwelcome energetic attachments.

Grounding, centering, cleansing, and shielding can all be done purely through guided meditation and visualization, though they can also be accomplished or enhanced with crystals, herbs, talismans, oils, energetically charged water, incense or other sacred smoke, salt, sigils, or magickal tools and techniques.

Let's try a basic cleansing, grounding, centering, and shielding meditation technique, then look at some variations on these techniques I've found useful and particularly relevant to my practice as a Sagittarius witch, and some thoughts on how to cultivate a daily spiritual hygiene practice you'll actually stick to.

Simple Cleansing, Grounding, Centering, and Shielding Meditation

This meditation doesn't require any magickal items apart from yourself. You only need a quiet place where you won't be disturbed for a few minutes.

Step 1: Cleansing

Close your eyes. Become aware of a spark of bright light within your core. As you inhale, feel it contract, and as you exhale, feel it expand. Each breath it contracts a little less and expands a little more. It starts as a spark, then becomes the size of a golf ball, then the size of a baseball, and so on. Everything that light touches will be purified and cleansed. Feel anything unwanted being burned away by the bright light. Keep breathing and expanding the ball of light until it encompasses your entire body, with some room to spare.

Step 2: Grounding

Stand if you're able. Breathe deeply and close your eyes. Visualize roots growing from the bottoms of your feet if you are standing, or your tailbone if you're sitting or lying down. The roots reach deeper and deeper, through the floor or ground, through rocks and stones, growing colder as they reach deeper into the earth. Eventually you will notice a shift in the energy, where it feels heavier or warmer. Once you feel this warm earth energy, draw it up through your roots, like you're sipping through a straw. Draw the energy up and up, back through the earth, until it reaches your feet or tailbone, and continue drawing it up through your whole body. Then send that energy upward through the highest point in your body, either through your raised hands or your head. Now feel branches reaching through your head or fingers, sending that energy upward, higher and higher, out into space, until you feel a shift in the energy, where it feels cool, bright, and/or crystalline. Draw that energy down, down, through the atmosphere, down through the sky, and into your body. Feel the energies from below and above intermix and mingle within yourself.

Step 3: Centering

Continuing directly from the grounding exercise and keeping your eyes closed, feel for a spot within your body that is the focal point of your consciousness in that moment. There are no wrong answers here, and that spot may change by the day or by the hour. Once you find it, send that focal point drifting throughout your body for a while, until you find a place where it feels comfortable and balanced. Breathe into that space.

Step 4: Shielding

Continuing from centering, still with your eyes closed, focus on that center point of your consciousness once more, and use your breath to expand it to surround yourself, as you did with the cleansing meditation. However, instead of visualizing it as a ball of light, imagine it as a protective barrier. It can be whatever makes sense to you—perhaps an energy bubble, maybe branches with thorns, maybe plexiglass, or a suit of armor. Use what works for you and experiment with different combinations. The most important piece is your focus and intent. If possible, speak your intention aloud. For example, "Protect me from *such-and-such thing.*" You may end with saying "I am protected" followed by "so mote it be," or "and so it is," or whatever phrase rings true with your practice.

Variations on Grounding and Centering for Specific Situations

Like many of my Sagittarius friends, I am an extrovert. I love meeting new people. I love to talk, laugh, share ideas, and tell and listen to stories. In my forties, however, I've definitely started living a more introverted lifestyle, avoiding most parties and social gatherings, even before the COVID-19 pandemic hit. Part of that is me becoming more okay with living inside my own head and body and enjoying my own company, part of it is because I can't stay up as late or drink as much as I did in my younger years and am losing interest in being around drunk people, and part of it is because my nature as a Sagittarius and as an empath means that I have a tendency to get overstimulated in social settings. To help alleviate or avoid this, I use a couple of different techniques.

Ground and Center within Yourself

When I'm around people I like, I tend to unconsciously mirror their energy a bit, and if I do this with a lot of different people in a short time period, I end up feeling as exhausted and confused as a chameleon in a bowl of Skittles. This is the case especially when I'm at multi-day conferences, festivals, or work retreats. One time when I was discussing this with Ivo Dominguez, Jr. between sessions at a conference, he taught me a technique that helps a lot before, after, and during gatherings: grounding and centering within yourself. This is my slightly simplified version of his technique.

Close your eyes and take several deep breaths. When your breath becomes deeper and slower, turn your attention to your third eye. Visualize an indigo spinning orb there, and pull your energy through it and deep into your head.

Find your inner temple. If you haven't developed one yet, visualize a comfortable and sacred place within yourself where you would feel content and at peace. Spend some time looking around.

Once you have a sense of your inner temple, ground and center *within that space*, using whichever technique works best for you. I usually go for the tree meditation described earlier in this chapter. Remember, you are not grounding within the Earthly plane in your physical body, but rather you are grounding within the plane held deep within your own consciousness, so it will feel a bit different from the usual grounding and centering exercise. Practice will help make it more intuitive over time.

Grounding Up to Quiet a Busy Brain

This is an alternate method of grounding I've experimented with. My brain is almost always busy, so calming it down and getting it to focus can be difficult. Sometimes my head feels so buzzy, I just can't manage to move my energy down into the earth effectively, and it's easier to let it take a path of less resistance by going *up* through my head instead of *down* through my feet. This meditation helps release excess energy and gives you the opportunity to table a lot of ideas, worries, and other brain activity, and let your higher Self sort them out and return them to you later, if needed.

Take several deep breaths and close your eyes.

Feel the busy-ness of your brain. Feel your center of consciousness focused in your head.

Now feel a tether connecting the top of your head with your higher Self, the part of you that is eternal. I usually visualize my higher Self as a speck of stardust in space, for example.

Now feel the crown of your head opening up, and push all those bouncing thoughts and busy-ness toward your higher Self. Feel those thoughts and energy being pulled through the cosmos. You may visualize this as a stream of ones and zeroes, thought bubbles, or a fire hose of chaotic information. Imagine your higher Self taking all these thoughts and sorting them out and processing them for you to retrieve later, perhaps with new inspiration or ideas for how to address them.

When you feel you've released enough, feel the top of your head close, and focus on your breathing once more.

Thoughts on Daily Practice

Most magickal teachers, myself included, emphasize the importance of grounding, centering, cleansing, and shielding daily, but I'm going to level with you: I have started and stopped more daily magickal practices than I can count. I know regular spiritual hygiene and magickal work are vital to helping me develop into the best Sagittarius witch I can be, but I am not great at sticking to a routine someone else tells me to do, or what I feel like I'm *supposed* to do. Doing the same exact thing every single day isn't something that comes naturally to fire signs, but don't worry—you can mix it up!

Pagan author Irene Glasse taught me the concept of having a daily practice menu of options to choose from. Come up with a list of things you'd like to do daily or regularly: meditation, grounding, centering, shielding, cleansing, saying a specific prayer, lighting a stick of incense or a candle for your helper spirits or ancestors, aligning your chakras, singing a chant, pulling a tarot card or three, blessing yourself, looking at the day's astrology, putting on specific pieces of magickal jewelry ... there are tons of possibilities. Each day, do whichever things on your menu that you have time for and feel like doing, but try to do at least one thing. It helps to have a default action for days you're feeling indecisive: a super easy thing that's pleasurable and takes less than a minute to do.

As I'm writing this, my current bare-minimum daily practice involves a grounding, centering, cleansing, and shielding meditation and a prayer to the helper spirits, allies, and divine beings I work with, which takes maybe one or two minutes to do. I do that before I even get out of bed. Even though I'm extremely *not* a morning person, I've found it's easiest for me to meditate if I commit to it as my first action of the day, before I let myself look at my phone. Most days I also do a few minutes of gentle yoga and pull a three-card tarot spread for the day. But on particularly busy days, or days where I have to get up early to travel, I cut myself some slack on doing yoga and tarot, since those things take longer. I also try to do some brief journaling at the end of my day with an app on my phone.

That may sound like a lot, but I didn't start doing all those bits of daily practice all at once. I started with just one thing and built onto it, and I regularly remove things from my practice if I no longer have motivation to do them or if I feel they aren't helping anymore.

If you struggle to find time alone to meditate, ground, center, cleanse, and shield, I suggest doing it while you're showering or bathing. You can even do something as quick as a brief elemental acknowledgment, focusing on how the various elements are present in your shower—the water and air surrounding you, obviously, but also the heat in the water for fire and the minerals in the water for earth—and blessing yourself with the powers of those elements.

The important thing is to create a practice you like and that you can stick to. Get some regular spiritual hygiene into your routine, but focus on what works for *you*, even if it's a different practice every day, and feel free to change up your routine when it gets stale.

Craft Your Own Travel Altar

Mama Gina

Oh, Sagittarius! You are well known for your desire to observe the world in your search for truth. You are the arrow that springs from the bow, and the journey that it takes. You pack light and might even have a go bag ready for those impromptu trips. Alas, the soul ruled by Jupiter sometimes lacks focus as you aim your sight for the bigger picture. Wherever you find yourself in need of centering, a tiny travel altar can be the perfect focal tool for the magickal Sagittarian.

Crafting your own travel altar allows you to honor your spiritual tradition and carefully choose each element of your roving ritual space. As you design, you might want to consider materials and items that will pack very small and that will not be damaged through repeated packing and unpacking. Be aware of flame and smoke restrictions as you consider items like candles or incense.

Two Simple Altars

A simple and discreet travel altar may be made from a four-inch to six-inch square of white silk or linen and fabric paints. Determine the placement of your elements and paint each section of the square in the color correspondences from your own tradition. A battery tealight for the center completes your altar.

If you wish to be a bit more extravagant, gather a four-inch to six-inch square of black or white fabric, a charm or item to represent each element or deity that you want to carry with you, as well as a box large enough to hold everything. If you are unsure where to start, try selecting a battery tealight for the element of fire, a tiny vial of blessed water for water, a small bell for air, and a pentacle charm or your favorite grounding stone for earth. Turquoise is an excellent soothing stone for Sagittarians. Place each item in its respective quarter and add a small charm of your patron deity as the perfect centerpiece for this altar.

Consecrate Your Altar

Before you travel, you may wish to direct your altar to its divine purpose.

Begin by lighting incense with a fragrance that will linger on the cloth. Each time you open your altar in the future, the scent will remind you of your intent. Frankincense or Dragon's Blood is quite inspirational for Sagittarian souls. Alternatively, ring a bell to set your divine space. Take three deep breaths and ground.

Lay your altar out as you might use it in the woods or in that future hotel room.

Turn on the travel-safe battery tealight and honor the flame that it represents.

State your intention.

By Sky and Spark, Sea and Sand,
With Spirit at the Heart,
I consecrate this altar.
Remind me of my Art!
By Air and Fire, Water, Earth
And all that is Divine,
That I may know the Magic
In every road unwinds.

Once finished, turn off your tealight, pack up your altar, place it directly into your go bag, and take the magick with you!

WHAT SETS A SAGITTARIUS OFF, AND HOW TO RECOVER

Enfys J. Book

Sometimes, the world tries our patience. Sometimes, our hotheaded nature gets the better of us, and we say or do things we regret later.

Let's look at some Sagittarius witch pet peeves, and how we can deal with them constructively, as Sagittarians, instead of flying off the handle. We can lean into our natural qualities of curiosity and creativity can help us cope with these irritations.

Sagittarians Hate Being Lied To

We're honest people, and we tend to expect honesty from others. When we find out someone has lied, we feel betrayed. This goes double for people we're close to and leaders in our spiritual communities, because we tend to believe they are better, more reliable human beings than those outside our circle.

The Fix: Ask before Throwing Accusations

Take a breath and ask yourself: *How important was the lie, in the grand scheme of things?* Is it possible you misunderstood the person previously, or that they forgot what they'd previously said? Before you fly off the handle or go into full-tilt lawyer mode, assess if it's important enough to make a thing of it. If it's part of a pattern, or if it's about something very important, gather your thoughts and lean into your trademark Sagittarian curiosity by asking the other person questions before jumping to conclusions about their motives or their understanding of the situation. To keep it from being a hostile interrogation, start with phrases like, "Based on what you said previously, I understood ..." or "I may have remembered this wrong, but it seemed to me that ..."

And if it's someone you find lying to you repeatedly, take a hard look at that relationship and consider if it's worth continuing, or worth the amount of energy you put into it. We tend to value sincerity and trustworthiness, and it's okay to use that as a metric in evaluating who we choose to spend time and energy with.

Sagittarians Hate Being Ignored

We love being the center of attention, so when someone ignores us, it's tantamount to an attack. As an example, a couple of years ago, a friend ignored my text messages for ages when I was trying to get an update on something important they promised to do, and the frustration of being ignored kept me up at night for *weeks*.

The Fix: Be Patient, and Shift Your Perspective

In the case of my friend, when we did finally talk, I learned she was in a shame spiral around not doing the important thing, while also being uncertain how to start. I offered to join her on a video chat so we could talk through the process while she was doing it, and we got through the important thing together. I wish I'd used some of my Sagittarian creativity and curiosity to consider or ask about what kinds of things she might be going through, and I wish I'd offered concrete help sooner, rather than just asking her "Did you do this thing yet?" repeatedly.

If someone is ignoring you and it's driving you to distraction, don't immediately assume it's because you did something wrong or that they're being mean on purpose. It might have nothing to do with you at all. People get busy, and sometimes life is a lot and people can't be there for you all the time. Still, be honest with them about how you're hurt by being ignored. It may bring the real problem to the surface, and you can deal with it together, or at least empathize with it.

Sagittarians Hate Being Alone in Our Enthusiasm

Sagittarians are enthusiastic to a fault. I even describe myself as an "enthusiasm enthusiast" (a term I picked up from an episode of the TV show *Gravity Falls*).[3] But our enthusiasm has its limits, particularly when others we're working with don't share our vision or our passion. I have pulled a lot of weight for various spiritual and mundane groups over time, and my enthusiasm definitely wanes when I notice I'm the only one in the group who's coming up with ideas, driving us toward implementing them, picking up the balls other people drop, and putting in extra time to make our projects the best they can be. It makes me feel betrayed and deeply frustrated.

The Fix: Take the Group's Temperature, Readjust Expectations, and Know When It's Time to Go

There are a lot of reasons why a group may be lagging, and this is another place where we can lean into our Sagittarian curiosity and creativity to find a better solution than simply giving everyone a piece of your mind. Maybe you were so passionate about a project at the start and took on so many responsibilities that the rest of the group didn't feel like they had important or interesting ways to contribute. Maybe the

3. Alex Hirsch, creator, *Gravity Falls*, season 2, episode 14, "The Stanchurian Candidate," written by Alex Hirsch, Jeff Rowe, and Josh Weinstein, aired August 24, 2015, in broadcast syndication.

group members are dealing with some stressful life things that are sapping their enthusiasm reserves. Maybe there's a disconnect between what you want to do and what the rest of the group wants to do. Or maybe the group has simply run its course.

Think about the skills each group member brings to the table and the things they like to do. If you're in a leadership position, consider sending an anonymous short survey to the group, asking about what direction they want to go and what they most enjoy about being in the group. Then talk to each individual and find out what they most like to do and what they'd be willing to contribute. Spend more time listening than talking for a while, and see what you learn.

If you're feeling tapped out and frustrated, set some boundaries and take on less work, even if that means the group might fail at something. This can, of course, be tricky in a workplace situation, but it can also highlight underlying issues that need to be addressed. And if you're still feeling drained after decreasing your workload, it's probably time to move on to something else.

Sagittarians Hate Feeling Trapped

Sagittarians adapt well to change. I'd even go so far as to say we thrive on it. When things stay the same for too long, or when we're locked into a situation we can't easily leave (e.g., a marriage, a mortgage, kids, a job), we can get anxious and antsy and may consciously or unconsciously sabotage it. For example, I waited to buy my first house until I was in my early forties, because the idea of a mortgage actively terrified me. Being locked into one location for ages? Yikes!

The Fix: Find Ways to Add Variety to Your Life, Even When You're Committed to Something or Someone for a Long Time

We Sagittarians thrive on novelty and variety, but that doesn't mean we have to stay away from any kind of long-term commitment forever. Inevitably there will be parts of your life that hit some kind of stasis: getting into a long-term romantic relationship, owning a home, forming a business partnership, becoming a member of a spiritual group, having kids, or taking a job with long-term benefits that make it worth sticking around for the long haul. But just because one part of your life is stable or locked in, that doesn't mean *every* part of your life has to be.

In our spiritual lives, our fear of being trapped can lead us to dabble in magickal work with various open groups, or focus on solitary practice, rather than committing to a closed initiatory mystery tradition. That's not necessarily a bad thing, but it's good to examine your motives and see if you're able to accomplish your goals with the various groups you're working with, or if you need something more dedicated and focused over a longer period of time.

In my life, by using my Sagittarian creativity, I've found ways to be able to commit to things while keeping at bay my fears of being trapped. In my career, I tend to look for opportunities for me to experiment and evolve my role over time, which makes things interesting and keeps me from frantically job-hopping. In my spiritual life, I'm constantly reading new books and learning new perspectives and skills to apply to my magickal practice. And with my home, I find I'm really enjoying finding ways to make it more awesome, and learning all kinds of new DIY skills. You can add variety to your life in so many ways, even when you seem to be staying put.

Sagittarians Hate Being Bored

The Sagittarian fear of boredom can impact all aspects of our lives and cause us to make impulsive decisions. It can be particularly detrimental to our magickal practice. A lot of magick works best by repeating it daily or weekly, and you learn to get better at something the more you practice it. But practicing the same thing over and over can be absolute torture for us. For example, I have tried to learn to play at least eight different musical instruments in my life, and abandoned them because I didn't like to practice. I just wanted to be naturally good at it! There's a reason we Sagittarians have a rep for being dilettantes.

The Fix: Do the Boring Stuff in Short Bursts

Unfortunately, there are parts of life and magickal practice that are just going to be a bit boring, but they're still important. To make these bits of work easier to deal with, I have a couple of suggestions from my day job as a project manager.

There's a popular productivity method called the Pomodoro Technique, developed by Francesco Cirillo in the late 1980s. To use this technique, set a timer for twenty-five minutes and focus on the thing you need to do, without distractions, for that period of time. When the timer goes off, stop and take a five-minute break. After a few focused work sessions and five-minute breaks, take a longer break of fifteen minutes. Doing the boring stuff doesn't feel so insurmountable when you timebox it, and you can add a dash of Sagittarian social engagement by partnering with a friend or two so you can cheer each other on. I have two friends on the other side of the country, and whenever one of us is having trouble focusing, we'll hop into a group chat and say what we plan to do in the next twenty-five minutes, then report back afterward and congratulate each other when we get stuff done.

Another way you can coax yourself to do the boring stuff is to roll a twenty-sided die and commit to working on the boring stuff for the number of minutes you roll on the die. I find this works particularly well for cleaning and other chores. If you don't have a twenty-sided die, there are apps you can use to roll a virtual die or pick a random number between one and twenty.

Use Your Sagittarius Powers for Good

It's all too easy to let mundane bullshit get under your skin. The world has no shortage of annoyances, and people are gloriously flawed and don't always act the way we want them to. But we can overcome these obstacles by leaning into our Sun sign's better qualities of curiosity, passion for learning, and experimenting with new ideas and techniques.

Sagittarius Road Opener

Devin Hunter

Sagittarians are known for big personalities and big hearts, but we are also known for our big ideas. Big ideas, however, come with a lot of small details, and we definitely aren't known for being detail oriented. Every star sign has an Achilles heel, and this just happens to typically be ours, causing big blockages and seemingly insurmountable obstacles on our road to success.

It is all too easy for the mighty flames of a Sagittarian to be smothered by the chaotic flood of minutiae that follows our best ideas. The next time you have a big idea worth chasing, perform this working to help avoid the usual trappings and to clear your path of obstruction.

You will need:

- A journal and something to write with
- Your preferred divination system
- One golden candle
- Jupiter oil: Blend this oil on a Thursday during the hour of Jupiter. In a half-ounce bottle, add nine drops each of carnation essential oil and copal oil, along with three drops of oakmoss essential oil, and fill the rest of the bottle with a carrier oil (such as fractionated coconut oil).

Instructions:

After blending the Jupiter oil, take your journal and write out your big idea as though you were pitching it to an investor. Start off by summarizing it in three or four sentences, then underneath it, write out two to five sentences explaining each of the following: why you are excited by this idea and think you will be successful, how you plan on achieving your goal, and what spiritual/magickal support you need to make it happen.

Using your favorite divination method, perform a reading on each of the above sections of your pitch, seeking clarity on how to overcome obstacles related to it. Next, taking your readings into consideration, adjust your pitch where needed to include the information you've learned.

In a ritual setting of your choosing, anoint one golden candle with Jupiter oil and then invite your spirit allies (and ancestors) to join you. Call upon the power of our planetary ruler with the following invocation and then read your "pitch" aloud.

Invocation of Jupiter

Hail Jupiter Victor, who is victorious in all things!
Hail Jupiter Centumpeda, who makes stable all efforts!
Hail Jupiter Optimus Maximus, who is the greatest of all in creation!

I beseech you to hear my words and lend your strength. Through you no task is impossible, no goal unachievable. It is in your three names that I lift my voice!

When finished, hold the oil in your hands at heart level and ask Jupiter to remain a permanent fixture in your efforts at manifesting your goal and ask that the oil represent your connection to him. Allow the candle to burn out completely.

Anoint the top of your head each morning (or before similar workings) by rubbing a drop of oil into your scalp and visualizing a crown. Say, "By Jupiter my path is unblocked and my goals are blessed; opportunity and success are drawn to me! Hail Jupiter!"

A BRIEF BIO OF DION FORTUNE

* * *

Natalie Zaman

Priestess. Poet. Mentor. Medium. Writer. Teacher. Sagittarian. Dion Fortune was all these things.

Born Violet Mary Firth on December 6, 1890, in Llandudno, Wales, her father was a lawyer and her mother a Christian Science healer. Early on, her parents singled her out as curious, intense, and intellectual, and encouraged her talents. Young Violet had her first vision of Atlantis at four years old, and by the time she was fourteen, she'd published two books of poetry.

In 1910 she was attending the Studely Horticultural & Agricultural College for Women where she studied plants and farming techniques, engaged in innocent mischief—Violet confirmed (on personal investigation) that the infamous Warden Lillias Hamilton kept her teeth, not a glass eye, in the cup next to her bed—and stood up for fellow students. This last item led to a psychic altercation with Hamilton who was supposedly well versed in occult practices and hypnotism and using it to bully her charges. The attack—detailed in *Psychic Self-Defense*—left Violet weakened but determined to master what happened to her. So began her work in psychotherapy at the University of London, and her journey into the esoteric world.

Her studies brought her into the company of Dr. Theodore Moriarty, an occultist and medium. Her book *The Secrets of Dr. John Taverner* is a reflection of their work together. She became involved with Theosophy and the Order of the Golden Dawn and interacted with other luminary mystics of the time, including Moina Mathers and Aleister Crowley. She communed with beings she called Ascended Masters, downloading insight and knowledge. In 1924 she founded the Society of the Inner Light, which still exists today.

It was during this part of her esoteric journey that she became Dion Fortune. A play on the family motto created by her grandfather—*Deo non Fortuna* (God not Fate)—would be both her spiritual and pen name. Fortune wrote many books on occult and mystical practices, but she felt that storytelling was her true teaching tool: "It is because my novels are packed with such things as these (symbolism directed to the subconscious) that I want my students to take them seriously. *The*

Mystical Qabalah gives the theory, but the novels give the practice."[4]

Sagittarians love travel, but Dion Fortune never passed the borders of Britain. Astrally, however, she voyaged far. She was fascinated with Glastonbury, the gateway to Avalon, and her beloved Atlantis. The opening chapters of *Glastonbury of the Heart* take readers mile by mile, from London to Glastonbury, passing Stonehenge and into the blushing apple orchards of the West Country. I visited Glastonbury years ago, and through her prose, I was able to explore this sacred space once more.

In the shadow of the Tor, deep in the warren of graves in Glastonbury Cemetery, is her last resting place. It's unremarkable except that it's covered in a blanket of flowers that change as visitors leave tributes. I'm sure she's pleased to know that she's touched, and continues to touch, so many lives, for she'd always shared her work "in the hopes that those to whom the author is now a stranger may someday be her friends."[5]

4. Dion Fortune, *Moon Magic* (York Beach, ME: Weiser Books, 2003).
5. Violet Mary Firth, *More Violets: A Child's Thoughts on Nature in Verse and Prose*, 2nd ed. (London: Jarrod and Sons, 1920).

A Sampling of Sagittarius Occultists

ELEANOR "RAY" BONE

influential British Wiccan high priestess

(December 15, 1911)

MARGARET LUMLEY BROWN

writer, occultist, and psychic

(December 7, 1886)

MELITA DENNING

founding member of the Order of Bards, Ovates & Druids,
author, first female Grand Master of the Aurum Solis

(November 26, 1917)

EDITH WOODFORD GRIMES *DAFO*

member of the New Forest coven
and early associate of Gerald Gard

(December 18, 1887)

RONALD HUTTON

author, professor, and historian of religion,
folklore, and the contemporary Pagan movement

(December 19, 1953)

OBERON ZELL-RAVENHEART

author, sculptor, editor of *Green Egg* magazine,
cofounder of the Church of All Worlds

(November 30, 1942)

THE SWAY OF YOUR MOON SIGN

Ivo Dominguez, Jr.

The Moon is the reservoir of your emotions, thoughts, and all your experiences. The Moon guides your subconscious, your unconscious, and your instinctive response in the moment. The Moon serves as the author, narrator, and the musical score in the ongoing movie in your mind that summarizes and mythologizes your story. The Moon is like a scrying mirror, a sacred well, that gives answers to the question of the meaning of your life. The style and the perspective of your Moon sign shapes your story, a story that starts as a reflection of your Sun sign's impetus. The remembrance of your life events is a condensed subjective story, and it is your Moon sign that summarizes and categorizes the data stream of your life.

In witchcraft, the Moon is our connection and guide to the physical and energetic tides in nature, the astral plane, and other realities. The Moon in the heavens as it moves through signs and phases also pulls and pushes on your aura. The Moon in your birth chart reveals the intrinsic qualities and patterns in your aura, which affects the form your magick takes. Your Sun sign may be the source of your essence and power, but your Moon sign shows how you use that power in your magick. This chapter describes the twelve possible arrangements of Moon signs with a Sagittarius Sun and what each combination yields.

Moon in Aries

Having your Sun and Moon in fire signs ramps up your desire to be more active in all arenas of your life. Your abundant optimism and daring nature can take you far, but it would be wise to develop a habit of close observation and planning before jumping into action. People will look to you for leadership because you shine bright, and your love of freedom means you'd rather lead than follow. You do have to work on learning detachment from outcomes and becoming more self-observant. Your competitive drive can cause you difficulties. Learn how to be more diplomatic and compromise a bit more and you will do well.

Courage is something you value in yourself and others. Even when you disagree with someone's beliefs, if they are ardent in following their truth, you will feel respect for their daring choices while strongly disagreeing. Honesty and direct communication are what you prefer. Your default nature is convivial, so even when you offer criticism, people can tell that it is offered with sincerity. You speak with great surety and authority, which can be interpreted as arrogance. Change your language and you will engage in debate rather than mere conflict. Let your fire be one that warms rather than roasts and you'll be more effective at reaching your goals. When it comes to matters of love and friendship, you come on strong. Slow down a bit and let others catch up with how you are feeling. You have a big heart and love to shower affection on others. You fall in love frequently and declare it just as often, and it is your truth. Just make sure that people understand what you mean and share your expectations.

An Aries Moon easily stretches forth to connect with the energy of other beings. Your fiery qualities act to cleanse and protect your aura from picking up other people's emotional debris or being influenced by your environment. It is relatively easy for you to blend your energy with others and to separate cleanly. However, take care not to use up too much of your own energy or burn yourself out. Learning to sense your flow and to moderate it is essential. The energy field and magick of an Aries Moon tends to move and change faster than any other sign, but it is harder to hold to a specific task or shape. This can be overcome with self-awareness and practice.

Moon in Taurus

The fixed earth of this Moon adds practicality and attention to details to your broad Sagittarius view of the world. You can see many ways to implement your great ideas and aspirations, though you are more inclined to pass them on to others. You like starting things more than finishing them. You have a stronger need for comfort and security than most Sagittarians, so you will generally look before you leap. In matters of love and friendship, you are patient, lighthearted, and devoted. You try to see the best in people, which usually serves you well, but some people are not as they appear. Learn to manage the hurt or disappointment so that you don't give up your open and generous nature.

This Moon encourages you to stop and smell the roses. Allow yourself to revel in your Moon's Taurean sensuality. In astrology, the Moon is said to be exalted in Taurus, which means that it favors success and good fortune. For a Sagittarian, this combination also gives you more creativity in the arts and practical matters. You have an innate sense of how to create an atmosphere, event, or place that encourages others to enjoy the beauty of being alive. Creating an experience that you can share with others is the best medicine for you when you are feeling stuck in your life. You will be happier if you are a lifelong learner because skills and expanding your horizons feeds your soul.

A Taurus Moon generates an aura that is magnetic and pulls energy inward. You are good at raising energy for yourself and others in workings and rituals. This Moon also makes it easier to create strong shields and wards. If something does breach your shields or create some other type of energetic injury, get some healing help or the recovery may take longer than it should. Generally, people with a Taurus Moon have less flexibility in their aura. You can work toward improving your flexibility by infusing your aura with fire energy. Astral travel and other forms of soul travel are harder to begin with this Moon sign, so draw upon your Sagittarius fire to overcome this. However, once in motion, a stronger and more solid version of you travels than is true for most witches. This combination usually comes with a green thumb, a love of stones, or animal magick.

♊

Moon in Gemini

Sagittarius's enthusiastic energy combined with Gemini's gift for communication gives you charisma, flair, and a persuasive voice. Your words and actions easily shift between being serious, funny, charming, inspiring. Your excitement and big ideas are infectious and affect everyone near you. You do enjoy being in the spotlight, and its bright light does tend to follow you, so make sure you are using that attention for good purposes. A Gemini Moon encourages spontaneity and a wide and ever-expanding collection of interests to feed your curiosity. Being unconventional and audacious is your norm, so you are somewhat surprised when people point it out to you. You sometimes seem detached when you are very engaged emotionally. The double mutability of this combo makes it harder for people to make sense of your emotional expression.

Gemini gives you more adaptability but also overstimulates the Sagittarius desire to try new things and take on more activities. Both signs love to have fun, so be careful not to overbook yourself. You do actually need rest and you are mortal. The key to making this Sun-Moon combination work is to form the habit of reminding yourself of your goals so you can get back on track. Cultivating patience is essential, not just for your projects, but also for how you deal with others. You are very curious and know much about the world; however, you'd do well to look deep into yourself. Knowing who you are is just as important as knowledge of the world. Honor and integrity matter to you, and self-awareness is the key to both those virtues.

A Gemini Moon, like all the air Moons, makes it easier to engage in soul travel, psychism, and gives the aura greater flexibility. You are a quicksilver fire that seeks connection but not a merger with other beings and energies. When your aura reaches out and touches something, it can quickly read and copy the patterns it finds. A Gemini Moon gives the capacity to quickly adapt and respond to changing energy conditions in working magick or using the psychic senses. However, turbulent spiritual atmospheres are felt strongly and can be uncomfortable or cause harm. A wind can pick up and carry dust and debris, and the same is true for an aura. If you need to cleanse your energy, become still and the debris will simply fall out of your aura. This combo is often good at awakening talents in others and raising energy.

Moon in Cancer

You have high ideals, deep instincts, and a better understanding of human nature than most Sagittarians. Your head and your heart are on good speaking terms with each other. Your outgoing personality combines well with Cancer's nurturing nature. You get joy from seeing the ones you care about succeed, which is admirable. The Sagittarius need to be seen combined with a Cancer Moon means you need true closeness and intimacy with people to be genuinely happy. Be mindful that you do not let your emotions or your need for security rule your life. You have great potential that may not be realized unless you direct enough focus into your own aspirations and needs. You are often lucky or have last-minute opportunities that save the day, but it is unwise to rely on them.

You know what will do well, go viral, and attract public interest. This can serve you in business, politics, the arts, religion, or whatever else you like. You have an abundance of creativity, imagination, and intuition. The Cancer Moon needs stability, which will generally mean a need for financial security, that your Sagittarius Sun forgets to consider. You'll feel better about life if you invest the time and effort to create your personal sanctuary. To do this, you will need to focus more on practical matters and their implementation. If you don't have a splendid and inviting place to live in, your negative traits are more likely to come to the surface. If you can't periodically retreat into your sanctuary, you get moody. You also need a space where you can hang out with friends and loved ones.

A Cancer Moon gives the aura a magnetic pull that wants to merge with whatever is nearby. Imagine two drops of water growing closer until they barely touch and how they pull together to become one larger drop. The aura of a person with a Cancer Moon is more likely to retain the patterns and energies that it touches. This can be a good thing or a problem depending on what is absorbed. You must cleanse and purify yourself before and after magickal work whenever possible. Fire is your best tool for cleansing yourself. Infuse your aura with fire energy to purify yourself. One of the gifts that comes with this Moon is a capacity for healing touch that offers comfort while filling in and healing disruptions in other people's energy. You also have a gift with plants or animals.

Moon in Leo

Double the fire means that you can be the life of any party and that you are always noticed by people. You do have to be careful that your flamboyance and desire for shock value don't overwhelm people. It is easy for you to take charge and take up lots of space. Check yourself before you wreck yourself and be more aware of your impact on others. Although you are inherently confident, you do crave regular validation from others. The more you choose to shift the center of praise and focus to others, the more you will be seen as the magnificent being you are. You are strong willed and idealistic and have big dreams and the personal magnetism needed to manifest what you want. The fixed energy of Leo helps give you more perseverance and stability.

Underneath all that jovial energy there is a great deal of introspection and a search for higher purpose. You are serious about trying to fulfill your life's purposes. You want your life to be remembered for its achievements and impact on the world. You will set your feelings and everyone else's feelings aside to reach whatever pinnacle of accomplishment you are seeking. This can be seen as a cold aspect to your nature, but it is really white-hot purpose. You are equally committed to matters of the heart, though that may be harder for others to see. To keep life in balance, regularly ask yourself if you are being kind and generous. Your best legacy will be how you made people feel, not the many goals you have realized.

A Leo Moon easily stretches forth to connect with the energy of other beings, though a little bit less than Aries and Sagittarius. The fiery qualities cleanse and protect your aura from picking up other people's emotional debris or being influenced by your environment. It is relatively easy for you to blend your energy with others and to separate cleanly. The Leo Moon also makes it easier for you to find your center and stay centered. The fixed fire of Leo makes it easier to hold large amounts of energy that can be applied for individual and collective workings. You are particularly well suited to ritual leadership or at the role of being the primary shaper of energy in a working. You also have a gift for empowering magickal tools and people, and healing is about restoring lost vitality.

Moon in Virgo

The Virgo Moon is reserved, inward focused, and a planner while your Sagittarius Sun loves to explore, act on instinct, and live in an optimistic glow. When you find your way to the midpoint between the two signs you have the best of both. Virgo's attention to detail and methodical approach help bring those Sagittarius dreams into reality. Sagittarius's directness, risk-taking, and confident nature transform Virgo's self-criticism into tools for personal growth. When you don't find or maintain this equilibrium, you may find yourself blocked from making decisions, pushing away the people you need, or using arrogance as a self-defense. This sounds challenging, but when you are in your sweet spot, you are wise, inspiring, and amazingly competent. Your observational and analytical skills connect small details to large structures with ease.

This combo brings out the most determined and individualistic traits of both signs. Although you know the rules of society and etiquette, part of you takes glee in bending those rules. This can be fun, but you'll get more joy from examining the rules you place upon yourself. You are often stricter with yourself than is wise. You can be very detached and impartial when you choose to be so, and that is when people will listen and heed your words. You get lost in your thoughts or overthink more than most Sagittarians. Since you are likely to be blunt at times, learn ways to patch up or reweave the bonds that get frayed. The one area where you may be pessimistic is in matters of love and friendship. Don't give up because you do need people to anchor you and uphold you.

A Virgo Moon generates an aura that is magnetic and pulls energy inward. This Moon makes it easier to create strong thoughtforms and energy constructs. You have strong shields but if breached your shields will tend to hang on to the pattern of injury; get some healing help or the recovery may take longer than it should. Virgo Moons are best at perceiving and understanding patterns and process in auras, energy, spells, and so on. You can be quite good at spotting what is off and finding a way to remedy the situation. This gives the potential to do healing work and curse breaking among other things. This Moon's mutable earth combined with Sagittarius's mutable fire can give you gifts related to crystal magick and opening portals.

♎

Moon in Libra

You are ingenious, animated, and become passionate about a great many people and things. You must be careful not to get carried away by your enthusiasm or you will spread your efforts too thin. You know how to be a friend and how to show that you care. This combo gives great charm and warmth to the personality. Your positive stance on the world is not always realistic, more aspirational, but this allows you to better the world by trying to make the ideal into the real. When the world disappoints you, it takes some effort to find your way back to your proper balance. Listen to everyone; it is all information, but it only becomes wisdom after you've placed it into context. You also have a talent for diplomacy, so strengthen your mediation skills and leadership roles will be more comfortable.

This combo can produce a tendency to slow decision-making and/or procrastinate. Make sure you attend to practical matters, budgets, and your work life. You have the skills to do well in the world but tend to be more interested in things that provide less income. You need to reassess your priorities regularly to ensure a proper balance. You are likely to have as many people as you want in your life, but to have an inner circle that truly sees you, you'll need to do more. Try letting people know that you are also sentimental and a true romantic at heart. Be mindful that your friendly and generous energy may be misunderstood as a positive response to someone's flirtation. Be clear and verbalize your boundaries and intentions. Although not impossible, your friends and lovers need to share some of your core spiritual or political beliefs or long-term relationships will be difficult.

A Libra Moon makes it easier to engage in soul travel and psychism and gives the aura greater flexibility. When you are working well with your Libra Moon, you can make yourself a neutral and clear channel for information from spirits and other entities. You are also able to tune in to unspoken requests when doing divinatory work. The auras of people with Libra Moon are very capable at bridging and equalizing differences between the subtle bodies of groups of people. This allows you to bring order and harmony to energies raised and shaped in a group ritual. You may have a talent for communication with animals, plants, and spirits.

Moon in Scorpio

You are clever, ambitious, determined, and don't mind being a rebel and out of step with the crowd. This tends to make you a leader or a trendsetter rather than an outsider. Mutable fire plus fixed water tends to make everything feel deeply personal. Learn to be more objective and strive to walk away from engaging in petty struggles. When you apply that drive to reaching your goals, nothing can stop you. This combination gives great fortitude, but learning diplomacy and subtle persuasion will take you farther. You are very independent and often assume that you are right. You often are right in your assessments, but not always. Your personal growth depends on expanding your perspective to include facts and perspectives that are new to you. Your memory and grasp of complex concepts is swift and incisive so you can learn almost anything you choose. This is especially true for occult or philosophical matters.

You have a strong survival instinct, which means that sometimes you will put your principles aside and choose pragmatism. You see deeply into other people; use this for mutually positive aims, not just identifying weaknesses. A Scorpio Moon puts up a wall around you so that you need to make a choice to laugh and let people see your lighter side. When you let your Sagittarius fire light up those Scorpio waters, you become like a magnet pulling people to you. You'll always have people around you when you want them. The people closest to you need to have strong and solid personalities to ensure respect and balance in your relationships. You will probably have several lifelong or long-term friendships or relationships. You love to dream and do better with fellow dreamers. This can lead you to become involved in campaigns, causes, and movements.

A Scorpio Moon gives the aura a magnetic pull that wants to merge with whatever is nearby. You easily absorb information about other people, spirits, places, and so on. If you are not careful, the information and the emotions will loop and repeat in your mind. To release what you have picked up, acknowledge what you perceive and then reframe its meaning in your own words. The magick of a Scorpio Moon is adept at probing and moving past barriers, shields, and wards. This also gives you the power to remove things that should not be present. Sagittarius's fire mixed with Scorpio's water also grant the capacity to read the energy of objects and places or imprint your energy into them.

Moon in Sagittarius

You are open-minded, playful, philosophical, hopeful, and a lover of humanity. You wear both horns and halos every day as you are both an imp and an angel with the changing of your moods. Geeking out on your newest favorite interest and telling the world it is amazing is one of your signature moves. All fields of knowledge, culture, and art catch your attention. You have an abundance of energy to connect every detail you see to larger overarching principles. You are outspoken and would have a hard time bottling up your thoughts or feelings. You don't mean to be blunt, but you will be unless you learn to pause before blurting out your thoughts. Once you sort this out, your double Sagittarius nature leads you to shine your light by showing others all the possibilities the world has to offer. At heart, you are an activist, a reformer who wants to bring about a better world for all.

Your weak spots are a tendency to be impulsive, to deny negative facts, and to expect too much of people. Develop a more objective view of the world; it'll feel like pessimism to you at first. You are highly adaptable and quick-witted, so even if you drop the ball occasionally, you'll pick it up and recover. If you are being blocked by someone, turn on your warmth, charm, and the twinkle in your eye and most people will let you get your way. Travel and new experiences are the best way to recharge yourself. You can feel at home almost anywhere and will have a wide array of friends. You are affectionate and kind, but not especially romantic. Your partners need to love adventure as much as you do.

The auras of people with Sagittarius Moon are the most adaptable of the fire Moons. Your energy can reach far and change its shape easily. You are particularly good at affecting other people's energy or the energy of a place. Like the other fire Moons, your aura is good at cleansing itself, but it is not automatic and requires your conscious choice. This is because the mutable fire of Sagittarius is changeable and can go from a small ember to a pillar of fire that reaches the sky. It is important that you manage your energy, so it is somewhere between the extremes of almost out and furious inferno. Your health depends on proper energy management and learning some form of meditation.

Moon in Capricorn

This earthy Moon helps make you more grounded and practical than most others of your Sun sign. You have a strong sense of purpose and enough self-discipline to tackle almost anything. You are more serious and self-sufficient than most Sagittarius Sun people. You like tackling large tasks and being responsible to prove yourself. Much of your success comes from the planning, plotting, and analysis that a Capricorn Moon loves. The downside to this gift is that you can be too serious and prone to worry and self-criticism. You feel most alive and more secure when you are working hard on your next goal. This is good, but so is rest and fun. Schedule time for recreation, and when people praise you, listen to them. Cut yourself some slack and you'll improve faster. Find the middle point between Capricorn's

Saturn influence and Sagittarius's expansive Jupiter rulership.

Over time, people will grow to admire you and what you've accomplished. You will change your goals and path several times in your life. This is normal for you and not a failing. Indeed, sticking to your first aspirations and goals would be a mistake. You evolve over time. Be mindful of how big an impact your moods have on others. Your personal standards apply to you and not to others. You'll have fewer unnecessary conflicts when you understand people on their own terms. You tend to give the impression of being strong and stoic, but make sure you let your friends and loved ones know that you need support just like everyone else. Mutual support and reciprocity are essential to happiness in your relationships. You are unlikely to have a normal personal life and that is okay. Create a home and a family of choice that suits you, not what society tries to enforce.

A Capricorn Moon generates an aura that is magnetic and pulls energy inward. What you draw to yourself tends to stick and solidify, so be wary, especially when doing healing work or cleansings. The magick of a Capricorn Moon is excellent at imposing a pattern or creating a container in a working. Your spells and workings tend to be durable. You also have a knack for building wards and doing protective magick. With proper training, you are good at manifesting the things you need. Fire contained by this earthy Moon also gives you remarkable stamina in workings and rituals.

♒

Moon in Aquarius

You tend to pursue high levels of stimulation with this Moon. The air of Aquarius fans your flame to keep you very active, constantly seeking new experiences, and always ready to debate any issue. Your imagination is powerful, and if you can create it in your mind, you can find a way to make it happen in the world. You have an aptitude for finding the steps that transform an idea into reality. Aquarius makes you more idealistic and ideological, which, when combined with Sagittarius's need for preaching, can lead to monologues or rants depending on the listener's perspective. Take care that you pick the right time, place, and audience for these passionate speeches so that you will inspire people rather than rub them the wrong way. You are a good storyteller, and stories often work better than rhetoric. Take care to apply your ethics to your power of persuasion or your enthusiasm may entice you to stray from what is right.

You'd do well as a teacher, counselor, coach, or in any situation that calls for imparting knowledge and helping people find their personal best. You love to look for deeper meanings in everything. Most people with this combination value diversity of every kind and are champions for creating a more open society. Make it a practice to observe thoughts and your life and consider them with detachment. It is a little too easy for you to get worked up and then drama will follow. This can be managed by self-awareness, which will result in self-regulation. Make sure you find partners and close friends who can keep up or learn to look back and check in on them. They also need to be willing to give you the freedom you need.

Your Aquarius Moon encourages a highly mobile and flexible aura. Without a strong focus, the power of an air subtle body becomes scattered and diffuse. When you have an air Moon, an emphasis should be placed on finding and focusing on your center of energy. Grounding is important, but focusing on your core and center is more important. From that center you can strengthen and stabilize your power. People with Aquarius Moon are good at shaping and holding a specific thoughtform or energy pattern and transferring it to other people or into objects. The fiery energy of Sagittarius also allows you to project your thoughts, feelings, images, and such for significant distances.

Moon in Pisces

Mutable water mixed with mutable fire makes you more easily affected by the world around you. You need to guard your heart because you feel deeply and are easily and equally hurt by thoughtless actions or intentional cruelty to yourself or what you observe. Thicken your skin, and put up some shields, but don't harden your beautiful heart. You do better when you have lots of people in your life. A circle of friends is your best defense and medicine against the harshness of the world. You are very psychic and live with one foot on Earth and one foot in the other realms. Use this gift to protect yourself from those whose hearts are not as true as yours. You can offer sympathy and help without being dragged down by others.

You have deep wellsprings of creativity that can be applied in the arts, the sciences, or in business. You do better if you work in a structured environment with real deadlines or you may find yourself adrift. If you choose to work for yourself, make sure you have detailed plans and procedures. If you don't have enough opportunity for self-expression or block the flow, it can turn into fretting and brooding. When you lose your balance, this combo creates dramatic emotional states and poor choices. Doing charitable work, being a volunteer, or serving your community help recenter and ground you. Don't worry about getting your heart's desire and finding that having it is not as wonderful as pursuing it. You will never run out of desires and goals. In matters of the heart, let yourself be loved; love is supposed to be reciprocal.

With a Pisces Moon, the emphasis should be on learning to feel and control the rhythm of your energetic motion in your aura. Pisces Moon is the most likely to pick up and hang on to unwanted emotions or energies. Rippling your energy and bouncing things off the outer layers of your aura is a good defense. Be careful, develop good shielding practices, and make cleansing yourself and your home a regular practice. Pisces Moon means you are best at energizing, comforting, and healing disruptions in other people's auras. Your Sagittarius energy helps you use this Moon to create sacred space, perform insightful divination, lead people in past-life journeys, and reveal hidden spiritual influences. Mediumship may be one of your gifts, but set up protections and call allies before each session.

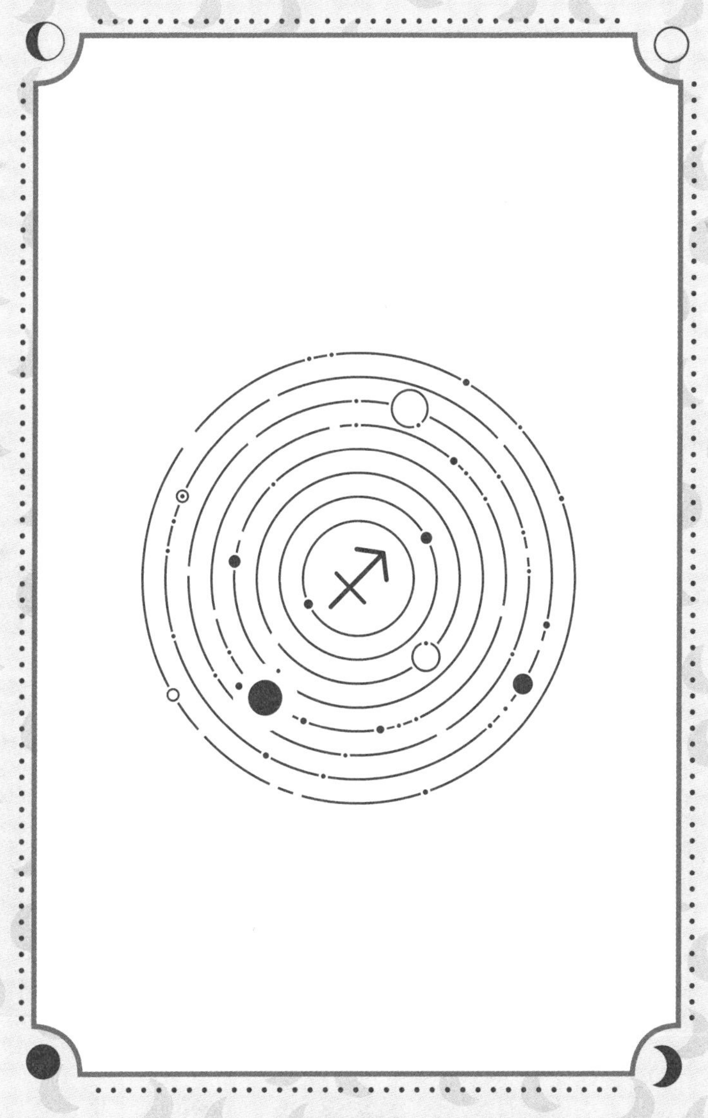

TAROT CORRESPONDENCES

You can use the tarot cards in your work as a Sagittarius witch for more than divination. They can be used as focal points in meditations and trance to connect with the power of your sign or element or to understand it more fully. They are great on your altar as an anchor for the powers you are calling. You can use the Minor Arcana cards to tap into Mercury, Moon, or Saturn in Sagittarius energy, even when they are in other signs in the heavens. If you take a picture of a card, shrink the image and print it out; you can fold it up and place it in spell bags or jars as an ingredient.

Sagittarius Major Arcana

Temperance

All the Fire Signs

The Ace of Wands

Sagittarius Minor Arcana

8 of Wands	Mercury in Sagittarius
9 of Wands	Moon in Sagittarius
10 of Wands	Saturn in Sagittarius

• MY MOST SAGITTARIUS WITCH MOMENT •

Enfys J. Book

Sometimes being a Sagittarius is like ... flip a switch and we're new people. People tell us what we've said or done in the past, and we don't even recognize it as ourselves. "Oh, geez, that thing I said (or did) last year? That was my beta release, that's not who I am today." We are masters of reinvention.

One of my most profound moments of reinvention came in my late thirties and early forties, which was a period of intense growth and opportunity for me. These years were also full of a lot of fiery anger, which boiled within me for far too long before I allowed it to catalyze an important spiritual rebirth.

Here's how the story starts. In the spring of 2018, my friend and covenmate Vickie, who was in her mid-forties, died suddenly of a heart attack. Though she wasn't a leader, she was an integral part of our coven's functioning, and her absence is still strongly felt. She was a selfless and generous soul, and I miss her a lot.

Everyone responds to grief differently. Though I was deeply sad about Vickie's passing, in typical fire sign fashion, some of my grief manifested as anger. I was angry at the fact that she wasn't around anymore. I was angry that I had to do more to support the coven in her absence when I was already super busy with my band, my job, and feeling constantly drained by an undiagnosed chronic illness.

All this happened around the same time I was coming to terms with my identity as a nonbinary person and deepening my knowledge of queering magick. My gender exploration and research on queering magick triggered a lot of anger in me as well: anger at the decades I spent pretending to be a woman because that seemed like the only option available, anger that so much of my magickal education leaned on binary concepts and language that I had accepted uncritically for years, and anger at always feeling like I didn't fit in. Being nonbinary often alienates you from both cisgender and transgender communities, much as being bisexual alienates you from both straight and gay communities; you're marginalized within a marginalized group. My anger was further fueled by the fact that I was not interested in expressing my gender in a stereotypical nonbinary fashion, which at the time would have meant making my gender presentation more masculine. My experience of being nonbinary is less about being in the middle of an imaginary continuum of *masculine* to *feminine,* and more like experiencing gender on a completely different axis altogether. All this frustration fed the grief and anger I was already feeling about my coven in light of Vickie's passing.

Unfortunately, expressing anger is something I'm still learning how to do in a healthy way. All that anger largely simmered below the surface inside me, eating away at me. I'd vent about it to my partners and close friends, but I couldn't bring myself to talk about any of it with my coven's leadership.

Then, in the summer of 2019, my coven's acting high priest left. At the time, our tradition's rules said that each coven must have two leaders of opposite binary genders, so his departure left a void that looked to be impossible to fill, seeing as the rest of our coven consisted of women and feminine-presenting people like myself. And my high priestess was struggling to run the coven by herself among all her other life responsibilities, and through her own grief. The future of the coven, which had been around since 2006, seemed to be approaching a crisis point in its thirteenth year of existence.

But then, like a switch flipping, something changed.

About a month after our acting high priest left, I took my first yin yoga class, and it happened to be during a full Moon. I have, historically, struggled with most yoga classes because my wrists have a tendency to get tendonitis. Yin yoga promised to be easier on my wrists than other forms of yoga, but I had no idea how life-changing that one class would be.

Yin yoga is not a workout. My teacher called it "meditating in shapes." The poses are floor-based, gentle, and intended to be held for at least two minutes, sometimes more. You're supposed to find the place in the stretch where you feel strain, pull back a bit, then hold that while breathing slowly and consciously. On a physiological level, it helps you deeply stretch your connective tissues and gently release muscle knots. On a meditative level, it's a profound experience of being fully present in your body.

On that day, the yoga room's overhead lights were off, and instead the space was lit by white fairy lights. There was ethereal music playing. Our teacher spoke for a few minutes about the purpose of yin yoga, and said that because it was a full Moon, we should choose an intention of something we were ready to begin releasing before the next new Moon.

I thought about it as we got into our first pose. What did I want to release? I'm not sure what spurred it, but I managed to finally admit my anger to myself, and realized how much it was holding me back. So, I chose to focus on that, and through the poses, and the breath, I called up the anger, felt it unfurl itself, and saw it for what it truly was: insecurity, grief, and fear of what the future held. So, I spent some time letting those feelings express themselves within my head and my heart. And during savasana, the final resting pose, I thanked those feelings for working to protect me, and I let them sink into the earth.

I left that class in a daze. Though I had put in very little physical effort during that hour, I felt like I'd just had a full-body massage, and I felt emotionally lighter than I had in ages.

That night, during my coven's Mabon ritual, I received a message from the deities we were working with that day, Amaethon and Braciaca. Both are Celtic harvest deities. During a guided meditation, I told Amaethon and Braciaca what I had planted and harvested already that year: a wildly successful Kickstarter that funded the creation and distribution of my band's third album, three new classes on magick I'd developed and presented, and a daily magickal practice I'd significantly rebooted, including getting back into daily meditation. The deities' reaction to my list was basically, "Okay, yes, that's all great, but you've also been leveling up in your leadership abilities." I responded, "Okay, cool, I guess." Then they said, "You need to ask to be the acting high priest of your coven. You have the skills your high priestess needs, and you should cocreate what this coven is and can become."

To my own surprise, in a classic Sagittarian switch-flip moment, after more than a year of being angry about the possibility of helping run my coven someday, feeling like that was a responsibility I was obligated to but did not want, suddenly I was not only *okay* with this idea, but convinced it was the *absolute right thing to do*. The fear and anger were gone and replaced with feelings of peace, clarity, and certainty.

After the meditation, my covenmates and I wrote on slips of paper something we'd planted that year and were in the process of harvesting. On mine, I wrote "new album" and "leadership" and burned it, as the others did, in a shared cauldron. Interestingly, my high priestess's paper did not catch fire very well until I threw mine in the cauldron, and my paper lit hers. Later, she told me that the message *she'd* received in the meditation was that she needed to be ready to pass the torch . . . so I lit that torch for her, metaphorically.

I spoke with my high priestess privately after the ritual, telling her what I'd experienced, the messages I heard, and adding onto it: "I'm nonbinary. If the only thing standing between me and the title of acting high priest is a penis, that's stupid." To my surprise, she agreed, and said she would talk to our tradition's leadership and let them know she'd decided I would be her new acting high priest.

I wrote in my journal the next day: "Suddenly the idea of leading a coven, on top of everything else I have going on, isn't so terrifying. I think I can structure my life so it's not as big of a drain, and I think I can make my coven better … I couldn't sleep at all last night. My head was full of ideas and it felt like my aura was on fire with passion and excitement and a bit of trepidation. I ended up staying up late and writing a long list of ideas for next year's classes and rituals, and then I just kept thinking about it."

The next weekend, I was part of a large ritual with my tradition called Climbing the Tree, in which participants travel through ten different stations, each representing a sphere in the Qabalistic Tree of Life. I was aspecting (a form of divine possession) the sphere Chesed, which is aligned with Sagittarius's ruling planet, Jupiter. Chesed, like Jupiter, has expansive energy, all about seeing the big picture and making big changes. After channeling Chesed's energy during two multi-hour rituals, I later recognized that my work with Chesed and Jupiter over the previous several weeks preparing for the ritual was partly responsible for my willingness and passion for taking on this new leadership role.

As I lean deeper into the strengths of my Sun sign, I remember my experience of being so angry for so long, only to have that anger dissipate in the course of a single yin yoga practice. I had been too angry and arrogant to see the possibilities of how I could help change things for the better, or to even open my eyes and heart to the *opportunity* to change things. I was so convinced I knew what to expect and how things would go, I almost missed out on an incredible growth opportunity and the chance to make positive changes in my life and the lives of others in my coven and tradition. I had been leaning into the destructive side of fire, rather than the positive catalyzing force of fire, but once I flipped the switch from the former into the latter, things fell into place.

Since I took on the leadership role in my coven, I've helped rewrite my tradition's charter so that covens may have two leaders of any gender, instead of one male high priest and one female high priestess. I wrote and published a book on queer Qabala to help more queer people find an authentic spiritual practice that embraces nonbinary, nonheteronormative possibilities, and am working on its sequel. I've started writing another book on queer magickal practice and became the second author on this book you're reading right now.

New possibilities keep opening up because I let go of my anger and stepped boldly into a new future by saying *yes* to an opportunity in the spirit of our ruling planet Jupiter. Like the Fool of the Major Arcana, and like a true Sagittarius aiming their bow and arrow in the direction they want to proceed, I boldly took the leap into a new future for myself and my community. And I'm so glad that I did.

YOUR RISING SIGN'S INFLUENCE

Ivo Dominguez, Jr.

The rising sign, also known as the ascendant, is the sign that was rising on the eastern horizon at the time and place of your birth. In the birth chart, it is on the left side of the chart on the horizontal line that divides the upper and lower halves of the chart. Your rising sign is also the cusp of your first house. It is often said that the rising sign is the mask that you wear to the world, but it is much more than that. It is also the portal through which you experience the world. The sign of your ascendant colors and filters those experiences. Additionally, when people first meet you, they meet your rising sign. This means that they interact with you based on their perception of that sign rather than your Sun sign. This in turn has an impact on you and how you view yourself. As they get to know you over time, they'll meet you as your Sun sign. Your ascendant is like the colorful clouds that hide the Sun at dawn, and as the Sun continues to rise it is revealed.

The rising sign will also have an influence on your physical appearance as well as your style of dress. To some degree, your voice, mannerisms, facial expressions, stance, and gait are also swayed by the sign of your ascendant. The building blocks of your public persona come from your rising sign. How you arrange those building blocks is guided by your Sun sign, but your Sun sign must work with what it has been given. For witches, the rising sign shows some of the qualities and foundations for the magickal personality you can construct. The magickal personality is much more than simply shifting into the right headspace, collecting ritual gear, lighting candles, and so on. The magickal persona is a construct that is developed through your magickal and spiritual practices to serve as an interface between different parts of the self. The magickal persona, also known as the magickal personality, can also act as a container or boundary so that the mundane and the magickal parts of a person's life can each have their own space. Your rising also gives clues about which magickal techniques will come naturally to you.

This chapter describes the twelve possible arrangements of rising signs with a Sagittarius Sun and what each combination produces. There are 144 possible kinds of Sagittarius when you take into consideration the Moon signs and rising signs. You may wish to reread the chapter on your Moon sign after reading about your rising sign so you can better understand these influences when they are merged.

Aries Rising

The fire of Sagittarius combines with an Aries to make you competitive, driven, courageous, and daring. This is a forceful combo with lofty aspirations, high energy, and a quick mind, but you need to be careful not to burn out. You may not run out of fire, but you may burn yourself or others if you don't learn to rein yourself in. Your honesty and directness are increased by this rising to the point that tact and diplomacy often go out the window. If it weren't for your warm personality, you'd be in trouble all the time. You have a pioneering spirit that is drawn to the new, the edges of what is known, and being present at the beginning of grand ventures.

When you lose your cool, the results can be explosive. Learn to give small warnings so that people know when to give you space or to prepare. You want to inspire and guide people, and that will be harder if you seem erratic. You are quick to jump into friendships, romance, and relationships. You might be happier and more satisfied with your choices if you slow down the process. You do better when you have trusted friends and companions as they will help moderate your actions and emotions.

An Aries rising means that when you reach out to draw in power, fire will answer quickly and in abundance. If you need other types of energy, you need to reach farther, focus harder, and be more specific in your request. This combination makes it easier for you to summon and call forth spirits and powers and create bindings. The creation of servitors, sigils, amulets, and charms is favored as well. This rising also amplifies protective magick for yourself and others. You may have a talent for fire scrying.

Taurus Rising

A Taurus rising can bring a solidity and steadfast determination that complements Sagittarius optimism, though it also makes you a bit less active. You are more calm and practical than most other Sagittarians but also more hedonistic. You appreciate life and are good at reminding others that life is meant to be lived. You have a greater need for quiet times and a cozy home as well. You are good at finding ways to bring abundance to your life. You crave emotional stability and solid relationships; your success in the world often hinges on the people in your life. Gardening or walks in nature help you think more clearly.

You have good instincts for helping people discover their innate talents. You also know how to put people at ease. You have a knack for public relations, humanitarian work, commerce, and resource management. You can work in large organizations but only when you respect the leadership. Whether it is with children or adults, teaching or mentoring will be part of your life and possibly a profession. Working with people teaches you how to show your heart. As you get older, try to maintain or increase your level of physical activity. This is essential if you want to keep that Sagittarius fire bright and your body comfortable.

Taurus rising strengthens your aura and the capacity to maintain a more solid shape to your energy. This gives you stronger shields and allows you to create thoughtforms and spells that are longer lasting. This combination also makes you a better channel for other people's energy in group work because you can tolerate larger volumes of different types of energies. You have a powerful voice for invocations, trance work, and hypnosis. Your spiritual voice carries a long distance. This combo also makes it easier to work with nature spirits and plant spirits in particular.

♊

Gemini Rising

With this rising, you are even more talkative than most Sagittarians. You come across as bright, vivacious, and genuinely interested in the people around you. This keeps you in the loop for all the events and activities you want to attend. You can go from specific details to grand principles with ease, which makes it easier for you to understand and explain complex topics. You swing back and forth from being overly playful to being exceedingly serious. To bring balance, try knitting, painting, carving, playing a musical instrument, juggling, or anything that uses your hands in a skillful way. These sorts of activities greatly reduce stress and improve mental focus.

You love being in love, which is a wonderful thing if managed well. However, you have a hard time with commitment and don't quite know how to open your heart to others. Just make sure everyone is on the same page on how you set the rules of your relationship. Be patient with yourself, your friends, and your lovers. Thankfully your sense of joy always reasserts itself no matter the circumstances. Try to listen to the people in your life who are the practical planners who pay attention to the details that you glide past.

Gemini rising combines your Sagittarius insight to make you adept at writing spells and rituals. This rising helps your energy and aura stretch farther and to adapt to whatever it touches. You would do well to develop your receptive psychic skills as well as practices such as mediumship and channeling. This combination can also lend itself to communication with animals, plants, and spirits. You can pick up too much information and it can be overwhelming. Learn to close and control your awareness of other people's thoughts and feelings. You may have a gift for interpreting dreams and the words that come from oracles and seers.

Cancer Rising

You are more inwardly and outwardly emotional than most other Sagittarians. Nostalgic longings and sentimental attachments are strong in you as well. You show caring through material gestures such as food, presents, the gift of your time, or the opening of your heart. You don't always feel like others reciprocate and hold up their end of a friendship or a relationship. This is true some of the time, but it may also be that you do not understand how others who are different from you express caring. Choose to use your intellect so you are not ruled by your emotions and intuition. Don't be frustrated if it takes time to narrow down and select your life goals, because you have many options. However, do not expect the universe to send you clues and omens on what you should do; solve the riddle yourself.

You have a love of history, folklore, genealogy, museums, and such. This can bring you great joy and activities that you treasure your whole life. These interests may shape your career choices. You have a talent for giving good guidance, which could lead to a career or simply be your role in your peer group. You need to blow your own horn more often. In matters of love, you are tender, loving, and are more likely to focus on relationships than other Sagittarians.

Cancer grants the power to use your emotions, or the emotional energy of others, to power your witchcraft. You can draw on a wide range of energies to fuel your magick, but raising power through emotion is the simplest. You are good at dreamwork, emotional healing, or past-life recall. Moon magick works well for you as does work done by the ocean. Color magick—such as the choice of colors for candles, altar cloths, robes, banners, and color visualization—can also serve you well.

Leo Rising

When you enter a room, the energy shifts and most people look up. This is great when you feel like taking charge or being the center of attention, but that is not always true. Leo is ruled by the Sun, and you tend to create the emotional and spiritual weather around you. When you are not doing well, things turn stormy. You are a natural leader and often a good ensemble player as well. You espouse high ideals and philosophies, but keep an eye on yourself lest that double fire should lead you to arrogance or hubris. Focus on walking your talk and leading by example.

You love to be over the top in most things in your life. You tend to always think that more is better; it isn't. Be mindful that excesses can lead to health issues. You are a loyal friend and tend to forgive offenses swiftly. Be as kind to yourself as you are to others. In matters of love, remind yourself that the first flush of attraction and romance is not mature love. Give yourself time before making commitments.

For long-term friendships or relationships, you must admire the person more than you like or love them. That is your key to commitment.

Leo rising means that when you reach out to draw in power, fire will answer first. If you need other types of energy, you need to reach farther, focus harder, and be more specific in your request. Your aura and energy are brighter and steadier than most people's, so you attract the attention of spirits, deities, and so on. Whether or not showing up so clearly in the other worlds is a gift or a challenge is up to you. You may be good as an oracle or channeler. Your Sun and rising give you a knack for energy healing work.

Virgo Rising

This earthy and practical rising sign moderates your fire so that you can work harder and more efficiently in pursuit of your goals. You are a keen observer of the world that notices the pertinent details. You are more careful and take your time to do things properly. When you are doing well you are discerning, and when you are frustrated you become hypercritical. This criticism and censure may be aimed at others or at yourself. In either case, it is generally nonproductive and drains your forward momentum. Take a break, clear your head, and apply your substantial powers of analysis for finding positive approaches to your circumstances.

You are more modest than most Sagittarians, so you need to make a conscious effort to take pride in your accomplishments and the good you do. You are very gifted in many ways, but you hold such high standards you don't often see that you are remarkable. So long as you know your worth, no one can push you off balance. This is also important in matters of the heart so that you see yourself worthy of love and affection. This combination tends to produce highly spiritual people with a calling that can lead to serving as clergy.

Virgo rising with a Sagittarius Sun makes it easier to work with goddesses and gods who are connected to wisdom, civilization, agriculture, and crafts. You have a flair for creating guided visualizations that can work as spells of a sort. Divination, oracular work, and acting as a voice for spirits is favored. Be careful when you entwine your energy with someone else because you can pick up and retain their patterns and issues. Always cleanse your energy after doing solo or collective work. You have a gift for knot magick, wheat weaving charms, and braiding energy together in collective work.

♎

Libra Rising

You can become whatever is needed for any situation. You can be a politician, a preacher, a diplomat, a teacher, or whatever role is needed to be the right kind of persuader. You know how to sound, what to wear, and how to pull off all the little nonverbal cues of a culture, scene, or in-group. Your warmth can melt away most icy obstacles. You are better than most Sagittarians at finding the balance between being pushy and being a pushover. This combination can interfere with making decisions and overthinking your plans. Your quality of life will improve the faster you move from brainstorming and thinking to actually implementing the tasks that lead to your goals.

You have a great deal of personal charm and allure. You attract the interest and attention of many people. Be mindful in screening which ones you allow close to you and take care not to compromise too much. In choosing partners, let the initial intoxicating glow of attraction fade and see if there is love as well before formalizing relationships. The more your day-to-day life matches your aesthetics, the more vitality you will have. Also, your environment changes your moods, so controlling your environment goes a long way toward evening out your moods.

Libra rising with a Sagittarius Sun wants to express its magick through the expression of your creativity. You may carve and dress candles, create sumptuous altars, healing poppets, write chants, or create or curate amazing ritual wear. You also know how to bring together people who use different types of magick and arrange smooth collaborations. You are good at helping others cut energetic cords and release spiritual or emotional attachments that no longer are healthy. Working with sound in magick and healing, whether it be voice, singing bowls, percussion, or an instrument, is also one of your gifts.

Scorpio Rising

With this rising, you seem darker and edgier than other Sagittarians. You are more driven and have enormous amounts of energy and willpower. You know what you want, and you will do whatever is needed to get it. If you feel you are blocked from reaching your goals, your frustration can make matters worse. This combination can set up situations that cause you to be seen as aggressive, domineering, or insensitive. You have a deep intellect that offers solutions to almost any problem you see. However, you need to manage your emotions to let that insight shine through. Once, or ideally several, times a day, take deep breaths and recenter yourself. Stay centered and you'll be more effective and have allies and friends.

You are deeply perceptive and might do well as a lawyer, a therapist, a writer, and, of course, a witch. You are one of a kind in so many ways and are unforgettable. Sagittarius and Scorpio have different approaches to life, which creates an internal tension and perhaps an excess of passion. Look to the rest of your chart, your life experience, and input from friends to find the nuances so that you become more flexible. You are a bit more possessive than other Sagittarians, but you want freedom and autonomy for yourself. Keep that in mind when considering your friends and loved ones.

Scorpio rising makes your energy capable of pushing through most energetic barriers. You can dissolve illusion or bring down wards or shields and see through to the truth. You may have an aptitude for breaking curses and lifting oppressive spiritual atmospheres. You could be a seer but only if you learn emotional detachment. It is important that you do regular cleansing work for yourself. You are likely to end up doing messy work and you do not have a nonstick aura.

Sagittarius Rising

This combination is exuberant, playful, opinionated, and confident. You are an open book, which is mostly good, though sometimes you overshare or speak the truth too bluntly. The good news is that people are quick to forgive you. You have a double dose of the gifts and challenges of Sagittarius. Make this an advantage by choosing to listen more and speak less, accept your accountability in schemes gone awry, and defend those who are in need. You can easily attract friends, partners, comrades in causes, and so on. Your personality is one of your greatest assets; develop it well.

You love to travel and are equally interested in cultures, landscapes, and meeting new people. When you need to recharge, being outdoors is your best option, whether it be a city park, a backyard, or the seaside—what matters is that you have the sky above. You enjoy being fully present in your body to feel your fires flow. This may be sports, dancing, hiking, or any activity that moves your body and engages your senses. Be mindful that you offer affection and praise to others regularly as you forget to do so in your hectic life.

Your magick is stronger when you are standing outside on the ground. Your rising sign's fire can become a fiery arrow that goes where you will it to fly.

Skill in the use of candles, wands, or staves is favored by this combination. This is because you can push your energy and intentions into objects with ease. You have a talent for rituals and spells that call forth creativity, wisdom, and freedom. This combination gives access to lots of energy, but you can crash hard when you run out. Stop before you are tired. If you do astral travel or soul journeying, be sure all of you is back and in its proper place within you.

♑

Capricorn Rising

Ambition is strong in you, and you are methodical and relentless in your pursuit of success. You also have a sense of duty and obligation to serve the needs of your community or society. You are serious, dignified, and careful about the face you show. You enjoy the world as much as any other Sagittarian, but you do work harder and play less. You are very much an individual and judge the world by your personal code. It is easy for you to get so enthralled with your tasks that you neglect spending quality time with people who care about you. You can go long stretches without too much human contact, but without affection and positive regard, you'll begin to fade.

Life tends to be challenging for you, though you are often lucky and intelligent about your choices. However, you tend to be drawn to taking on sizeable goals and doing it the hard way. Be more open to accepting and enlisting help from others. In your personal life, this can make you an excellent friend or partner; just don't vanish into your work. Also, your partner needs to be very nurturing and wise to the hard façade you put up. You are drawn to intelligence and temperament more than physical features.

Capricorn rising creates an aura and energy field that is slow to come up to speed, but has amazing momentum once fully activated. Make it your habit to do some sort of energy work or physical warm-up exercises before engaging in witchcraft. Try working with crystals, stones, even geographic features like mountains as your magick blends well with them. Your rituals and spells benefit from having a structure and a plan of action. You are especially good at warding and spells to make long-term changes. You may have a gift for manipulating the flow of time.

Aquarius Rising

You radiate uniqueness, distinctiveness, and unconventionality and it takes effort to fly under the radar. You retain a fresh and youthful outlook throughout most of your life. You will make a difference in the world, but just give people some time to think through all the amazing and practical ideas you have to offer. Your weakness is that you become more rigid when under threat. Little changes in plans or schedules or misunderstandings in conversations can annoy you to the point of disruption. When you do lose your control and your cool, it is quite a memorable sight for all present.

This combination makes for original thinking and moments of genius. The Sagittarius side of this combination provides the enthusiasm and people skills to make those ideas real. You have a broader understanding of how the large systems of society and business work so you can apply your talents almost anywhere. When it comes to long-term partners, you need to have an intellectual and a physical connection. Your partner will also need to be more adaptable than you are to make things work. You need more alone time than most Sagittarians to stay on an even keel. Learn to let go of arguments and heated discussions as you often keep going when something is done and needs to be released.

Aquarius rising helps you consciously change the shape and density of your aura. This makes you a generalist who can adapt to many styles and forms of magick. Witchcraft focused on calling inspiration, creating community, and personal transformation are supported by this combination. Visualization can play an important role in your magick and meditations. If you aren't particularly good at visualization, then focus your gaze on objects on your altar related to your work. Aquarius rising is gifted at turning ideas onto reality.

Pisces Rising

There is an otherworldly feel to you that marks you as a dreamer, a visionary, and a witch. You are so immersed in your psychic perceptions that you can forget that you are psychic. You are guided and often protected, but don't make your spirit helpers work too hard. When you focus on the physical world and practical matters, your understanding is equally sharp. However, unless you make a conscious effort to do so, you do not pay close enough attention to mundane matters. You tend to bite off more than you can chew unless you use intellect and intuition equally.

Although you may be shy when you are young, over time your Sagittarius Sun will make you bolder and better able to stand up for yourself. You are affectionate and definitely enjoy romance with all the bells and whistles. Be cautious when opening your heart to friends or lovers as you prefer to only see their best qualities. Learn to experience the whole truth of their natures and choose carefully. Music, and the arts in general, is one of the best medicines for your body, mind, and spirit. It is important to have people in your life who are highly structured to help keep you on track and motivated.

Pisces rising connects your Sagittarius Sun with the other planes of reality. Your power as a witch flows when you do magick to open the gates to the other worlds and realms. You have a special gift for creating sacred space and blessing places. You can do astral travel, hedge riding, and soul travel in all its forms with some training and practice. You can help others open up their psychic gifts. Music, chanting, and/or dance also fuel your witchcraft. A gift for shape-shifting and casting glamours often comes with this combination.

A Dish Fit for a Sagittarius: Fiery Fusion Dal Taquitos

Dawn Aurora Hunt

* * *

This recipe fuses tender spicy red lentil dal with the fun convenience of crunchy taquitos. For you, dear Sagittarius, this flavor explosion is super easy to make but packed with spices, cheese, and crunch to satisfy all your cravings. The cheese brings in elements of joyful energy that soothe the warming, exotic spices. This creamy filling bakes to crispy perfection wrapped in a corn tortilla, which holds the power of the Sun and its regenerative powers to rise and set and rise again.

You can make dozens of these for a party to share with friends, or better yet, make dozens for yourself! Just freeze a batch or two for those nights when you need a pick-me-up or a quick meal.

Note: This recipe is inherently gluten-free and vegetarian. If your diet precludes you from eating dairy, you can substitute the cheese for vegan cheese, but do not omit the cheese as it not only adds texture but, when melted, acts as a binder for all the ingredients.

Ingredients:

- ½ cup red lentils, rinsed
- 1½ cups water
- 1 tablespoon olive oil
- ½ onion, finely diced
- 3 cloves garlic, minced
- 1 teaspoon fresh ginger, grated
- ½ teaspoon each: dried cinnamon, cumin, turmeric, cardamom, paprika
- 1 6-ounce can tomato paste
- ¼ cup water
- Juice from half a lemon
- Salt and pepper to taste
- 12 corn tortillas
- 1 cup crumbled Mexican cheese, such as Cotija or Manchego

Directions:

In a large saucepan, combine water and rinsed lentils. Gently simmer, uncovered, on medium heat for twenty minutes or until lentils are soft but not mushy. Meanwhile, in a medium skillet, heat olive oil on medium heat. Sauté the onions, garlic, and ginger until soft and translucent. Add all the species, salt and pepper, tomato paste, and water. Simmer until some of the liquid has evaporated. When the lentils are cooked, drain off most of the water, reserving about two tablespoons. Add the onion mixture to the cooked lentils and mix in the lemon juice. Remove from the heat and let cool for fifteen minutes before making your taquitos. If the lentil mixture is very wet, let it continue to simmer until more moisture has evaporated, leaving the lentil mixture a sturdier, pastier consistency. If the mixture is too wet, it will not hold in your taquitos.

Heat the oven to 425 degrees Fahrenheit. Line a baking sheet with parchment paper and set aside. On a clean work surface, spoon about two to three tablespoons of the lentil mixture across the center of a corn tortilla. Sprinkle with cheese. Tightly roll the tortilla around the mixture, creating a long cigar. Place the taquito gently on the prepared baking dish so that it does not come unrolled. Repeat with remaining tortillas. When all the taquitos are on the baking dish, spray the top of them with cooking spray and bake for twelve to fifteen minutes until slightly golden brown and crunchy. Some of the filling may ooze out; this is normal. Remove from the oven and let cool for about two minutes before serving.

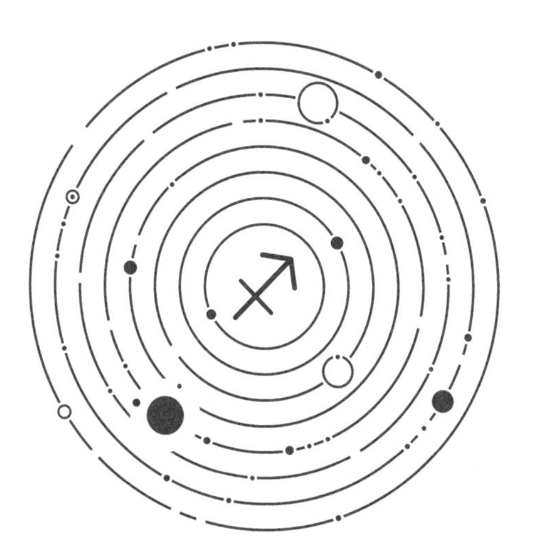

RECHARGING AND SELF-CARE

Enfys J. Book

Let's look at some ways to support your Sagittarius energy and help you become the best, most effective Sagittarius witch you can be. Intentional self-care is critical for us. But our version of self-care may look a little different from that of people in other Sun signs.

What Does Sagittarian Self-Care Look Like?

Sagittarians have a different definition of *rest* than other people. Recharging for us is more about immersive and varied stimulation than lying still. For example, I have never had much luck trying to nap in the middle of the day, but reading a suspenseful novel or going on a nature walk does a lot to recharge my batteries. I need something to engage my brain and my senses to relax.

When I was a teenager, a mental health professional said something I'll never forget: "Anxiety is the flip side of creativity." Sagittarius's active, passionate brain is great at making connections, which can lead to some amazingly creative art. It can also make us phenomenal strategic planners and problem-solvers, because we see things others miss. And we tend to be great networkers, connecting people who have some mutual interest for collaboration. Unfortunately, the scary underbelly of that quick-connecting brain is that we are also *fantastic* at worrying and thinking of worst-case scenarios. Because of this, mindfulness practice may be challenging for Sagittarians, but it is also crucial for our mental and physical health. If you haven't started a mindfulness practice, I highly recommend trying one.

If you're groaning at the mention of *mindfulness* and picturing a future yet-again failed attempt at building a meditation practice, I have good news for you: mindfulness doesn't just mean sitting still and meditating. It's a practice of being present in the moment and engaging your senses, even when you are doing something active. Here are several ways you can cultivate a mindfulness practice without sitting still with your eyes closed:

- **Mindful eating:** Focus on the tastes, smells, and textures of your food, truly savoring every bite.
- **Mindful walking:** Take a meditative walk through nature, tuning in to the feeling of your body

moving, the smell of the air, the feeling of sunlight on your face, and the sound of the birds and insects.
- **Mindful manual tasks:** Do something that keeps your hands busy, whether that's gardening, doing crafts, making art, painting a room, or cleaning. Fully immerse yourself in the task and how it feels.

A mindfulness practice is particularly useful for fire signs because it allows us to connect with earth energy that balances our natural fire. Earth energy helps us stay grounded and tuned in to the needs of our physical self, which we are sometimes very good at ignoring!

Another way to connect with earth energy is to build a relationship with the easiest-to-get crystal: salt. Since I moved to Maryland in 2005, I've discovered that spending time near or in salt water is fantastic for my physical, mental, and spiritual health. The salty air of an ocean beach resets my energetic bodies, and the sound of waves is so soothing. If you don't live near an ocean (or even if you do), consider adding a cup of salt to your bathwater to get a similar effect, or visit a salt room or float tank. Leaning into the earth element—particularly working with minerals, crystals, plants, incense, and other sensory experiences—can help us create the boundaries, wells of reserve, and groundedness we need to power and most effectively use our natural fire.

Divination to Bring More Balance to Your Life

The path of Sagittarius on the Qabalistic Tree of Life is the path of the Temperance card in the Major Arcana of the tarot, which typically features a calm figure pouring water between two cups, balancing the ebb and flow. Though I don't think many people would accuse Sagittarians of being innately balanced in any regard, the Temperance card gives us the key to *becoming* our best Sagittarian selves. This reading will help you find ways you can balance your life to become a happier, healthier Sagittarius witch.

Remove the Temperance card from the deck of your choosing and place it in the middle of your reading space, then shuffle the remaining cards. Focus on the question *How can I bring more healthy balance into my life?* and draw a card to place on each side of the Temperance card, starting to its right, then its left, then above, then below.

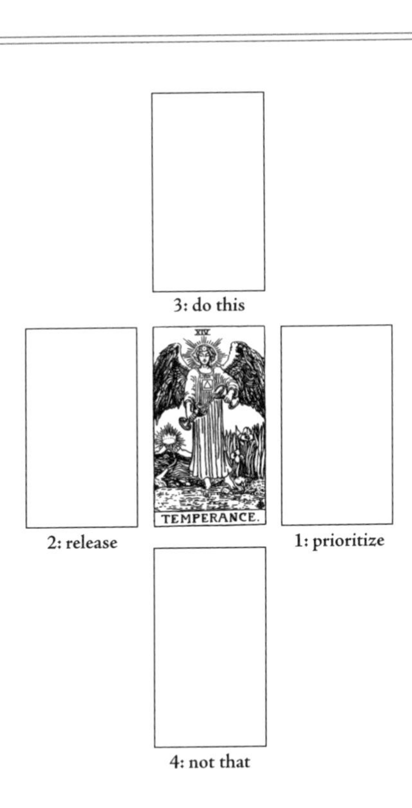

The cards laid down to the left and the right represent the big picture: what you should release and what you should prioritize. The cards on the top and bottom offer an immediate next step on how to go about prioritizing and releasing those things: a "do this, not that." For example, I pulled 1: Hanged Man, 2: Knight of Swords, 3: Ace of Wands, 4: 7 of Pentacles. To me, this means I should 1. prioritize shifting my perspective and be willing to go through a physical ordeal to connect better with myself and the universe, 2. stop indulging in a reckless desire to fix things quickly, 3. start by rekindling my passion and will with something new, and 4. avoid resting in satisfaction on what I've already done. As of this writing, I've been starting a new exercise regimen and taking concrete steps to add more vegetables to my diet, so this tells me I'm on the right track in focusing on long-term gains instead of short-term desires or things that seem like a quick fix, and that I should be open to new opportunities to do even more to rebuild healthy habits in my life.

(Side note: if, in the process of doing this reading, your cat knocks your tarot deck off the table, like my cat did in one of my test reads, then the message is that you should pay more attention to your cat.)

Earth Influences Make Us Healthier, Better Witches

Like witches of all other Sun signs, we are at our best when we lean into the sign immediately following our own, and at our worst when we lean into the sign immediately preceding ours. For Sagittarians, this means we are at our best when we lean into earthy, stubborn, tenacious Capricorn traits. If you combine our ambition with Cap's get-it-done focus and perseverance, we can change the world. If we lean back into dark, secretive, emotional Scorpio, though, all our bubbly energy gets directed into political sniping, grudges, and cynicism, which isn't a good look for us.

If you have any planets in Capricorn in your chart, consider how you can tap into that influence to help balance and empower your Sagittarius Sun. If you don't have any planets in Capricorn in your chart, look at the house or houses where Capricorn shows up, and consider how you can connect with Capricorn's energy in those areas of your life. In my chart, I have Venus in Capricorn, for example, so I tend to feel my best when I prioritize my love life and romantic partners. I also tend to express my affection with gifts (mostly silly memes I send to those I think will enjoy them). Because Capricorn touches the seventh and eighth houses on my chart, I thrive when I do regular, practical work to nurture the individual relationships I most value, and when I pay attention to how I use money in my life.

Earthy influences can dramatically improve our magick and our own health. Reaching for Capricorn energy can help lend focus and perseverance to our magickal and mundane work, which will make our efforts more effective, and ultimately more satisfying. Capricorn's grounding influence can also keep us from taking on too many different projects, and instead help us prioritize our body's physical needs for rest, nourishment, and enjoyable physical activity.

And speaking of enjoyable physical activities, let's talk about sex! Sexual activities, either with others or solo, can also be a great stress reliever and mood booster for us mutable fire folk. Most Sagittarians I know love good sex, especially when it's creative, when it involves all our senses, and even (especially) when it's a bit silly. Taking the time to regularly engage in solo and/or partnered sex, if that's something you're interested in, can simultaneously help keep you connected to your physical self and help keep your inner fires burning.

All that being said, though, there is such a thing as "too much earth energy," and Sagittarians are known for overdoing some of those earthy, sensual pleasures. In particular, we have a tendency to overindulge in delicious-yet-lacking-in-nutrients food and drink, which can sometimes lead to more stress in the form of health problems. We tend to have issues with our livers, gallbladders, and metabolisms, and some of that can stem from our food and beverage choices over the long-term. Mindful eating and focusing on foods and drinks that are both pleasurable to consume and beneficial to our health can curb some of the more self-destructive habits of overconsuming things that are difficult for our bodies to process in a healthy way. I'm not advocating following a diet or avoiding your favorite foods—diet culture and fatphobia have caused far too much damage in our society as it is, and I will not contribute to it—but I *am* advocating cultivating a mindful relationship with and listening to your body and its unique needs, including food, hydration, activity, and rest.

In addition to focusing on your body, take some time to consider two very important earth-driven aspects of your life: where you live and how you earn money. Your relationship with your home, the land you live on, and your sources (and quantity) of money all have a huge impact on your quality of life and are often our top sources of stress. Frankly, a lot of us are strapped for cash and living in subpar living situations, and all the mindfulness in the world isn't going to change that. I don't have any one-size-fits-all advice to give here, because everyone's situation has its own unique challenges and this subject deserves a lot more attention than I can possibly include in this little chapter. I will simply recommend some books that may be helpful for you:

- *Twist Your Fate: Manifest Success with Astrology and Tarot* by Theresa Reed
- *Make Magic of Your Life: Passion, Purpose, and the Power of Desire* by T. Thorn Coyle

Paying attention to our relationship with the earthy parts of our existence—how we treat our bodies, where we live, how we earn money—is fundamental to our overall health and well-being. Taking care of ourselves as Sagittarians isn't about dousing our natural fire with earth, but rather using the influence of earth energy to build a solid base from which our fire can blaze more powerfully. We can and should honor our passions by offering them some focus and clarity, enjoy our experiences more by practicing mindfulness, flourish with more healthy balance in our lives, optimize our living and job situations, and recharge in ways that make sense for us.

Sagittarian Self-Care Magic

Donyelle Headington

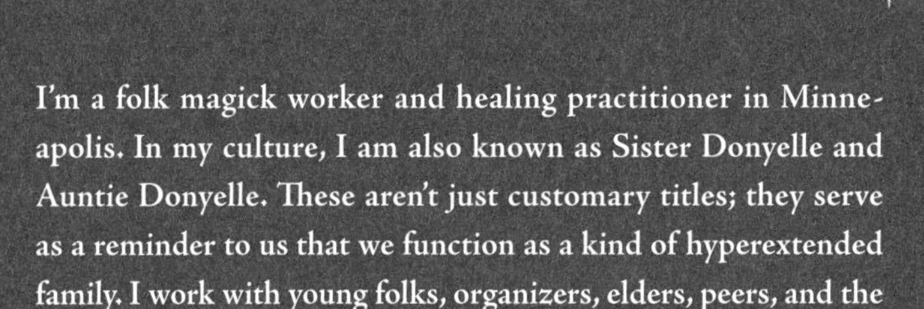

I'm a folk magick worker and healing practitioner in Minneapolis. In my culture, I am also known as Sister Donyelle and Auntie Donyelle. These aren't just customary titles; they serve as a reminder to us that we function as a kind of hyperextended family. I work with young folks, organizers, elders, peers, and the community in general around ancestral healing, trauma, and grief work. The following is my story of self-care in difficult times.

My city burned during the uprising that followed the murder of George Floyd. COVID-19 took the lives of so many elders, mothers, fathers, and children, that it seemed every day we were getting news of another community member's death. The toll on the mental health of my community was staggering. I found myself grieving daily around the events happening in the outside world, my inner world, but also, grieving my inability to plan and execute rituals, community events, and ceremonies to address the needs of my little village.

This trauma was fueling my Jupiter-ruled heart, and I was compulsively planning large-scale healing events. I knew just what to do, what was needed; I had the knowledge, experience, and connections to help address this growing need, but the kicker was, I was in as much need as everyone else. I didn't have the physical, mental, spiritual, or emotional recourses to make anything happen. I was forced to sit my behind down and work on myself. What was I supposed to do with all this big creative Sagittarian energy? Traveling and gatherings were out of the question, as COVID was in its first wave with no vaccine in sight, and the rise in violence in our city meant I couldn't be in my garden growing and building. I was entirely sick of Zoom happy hours.

I have a self-care practice I call my "building meditation," a step-by-step construction visualization I use to drift off to sleep. I visualize whatever structure I wanted to inhabit for the evening and slowly build it. Stone by stone, stud by stud, and beam by beam, until I fall into a sound sleep. I decided to expand this meditative practice to include anything I desired. In it, I go wherever I want, build whatever I want, visit whomever I want, and run off into the forest if I like.

It started as wish fulfilment, but quickly I realized that something more was happening. Some of these imaginings came into being. Minneapolis was having record gun violence. Every night I envisioned being in a safe crystal castle, away from the gunfire happening outside my windows. Then my family and I were invited to stay at a friend's pool house just outside town; it was built to look like a castle for their daughter. Now I'm not saying it was only my nightly meditations that brought about such a gorgeous outcome; some pretty powerful folks were praying us into a safer space. But when I walked into that pool house, above my head was the biggest, sparkliest crystal chandelier I had ever seen. It brought to life my visions of the crystal palace. Pure Sagittarian magick!

Don't Blame It on Your Sun Sign

Enfys J. Book

Some people wear their Sun sign as a mask. Have you ever met a Sagittarius who was just *so* Sagittarian? And they bring up their sign regularly in conversation? Chances are, that's not who they really are. They see their Sun sign as their destiny, or, worse, as a prison.

Every Sun sign has its laundry list of bad behaviors people attribute to it, and Sagittarius is no exception. Unfortunately, some people use their Sun sign as an excuse for being a jerk: "Oh, I'm a Sagittarius, that's just the way I am." But a Sun sign isn't destiny; it's opportunity. You have options and free will, and you have the power to lean into the good aspects of Sagittarius without taking them to their more destructive extremes.

Let's look at the negative Sagittarius stereotypes, and then examine how those bad behaviors can be twisted for the better with the help of some of the strengths of our Sun sign.

Sagittarians Are Arrogant

Sagittarians love to learn, study, and geek out about the things we're passionate about. But sometimes we believe we have all the answers, or at least, all the important ones. And in conversation with others, we may be so sure we're right that we end up being preachy or coming off as arrogant. Despite our mutable nature, we tend to dig in our heels in the face of disagreement, and may snap if we are proven wrong.

The Fix: Feed Your Curiosity

Famous Sagittarius Jane Fonda once said that the advice she wished she could give to her younger self was, "It's better to be interested than interesting."[6] Sagittarians may love to dispense wisdom to the point of annoyance, but we're also naturally curious and love to learn. If you catch yourself about to offer unsolicited wisdom or advice, take a conversational U-turn and instead ask some questions to get other people's perspectives and learn about their experiences. "Be curious, not judgmental."[7]

By the same token, when someone proves you wrong, instead of snapping back, employ your innate curiosity to

6. Belinda Luscombe, "10 Questions for Jane Fonda," *Time* Magazine, February 15, 2013, http://content.time.com/time/magazine/article/0,9171,2088024,00.html.
7. An anonymous quote often misattributed to poet Walt Whitman.

learn more about something you didn't understand as well as you thought you did. Ask questions.

Finally, as a general rule, make a point of reading widely and learning from a variety of different teachers so you can get different perspectives. When you are in a teaching role, remember that the best teachers learn from their students, and facilitate students learning from each other. And at the very least, keep this mantra in the back of your head: "I do not know everything and I do not have all the answers all the time."

Sagittarians Are Attention-Seekers

Sagittarians are the life of the party! We love a good joke, we love to laugh, we love entertaining our friends, and we love an audience. And unfortunately, that can turn into stealing the spotlight in less-than-healthy ways. I went through a phase in my late twenties where, every time I was at a party, I wanted to be the center of attention so badly, I ended up making an ass of myself. I'd drink a lot and lose any semblance of filter on the things that would go straight from my brain to my mouth without a moment of further consideration. And then I'd wake up in the middle of the night afterward, hating myself and worrying that my friends hated me, too.

The Fix: Use Your Star Power on Purpose

What ultimately helped me get over my bad party persona was joining a pirate band (yes, really) where I could wear a costume, play a character, perform, and be the center of attention on purpose, and regularly. It was a great way to channel my natural love of the spotlight into something that brought delight, rather than annoyance, to others—well, except for those who didn't like pirate music or the frequent bad puns we made as part of our act, but there's no accounting for taste. Of course, pirate band availability may vary depending on your region (though, heck, you can start one; I'm certainly not going to stop you!), but if you find yourself wanting to channel your love of performance into something more fun than being That Guy at parties, think about other ways you might be able to regularly perform, write, teach, or create visual art for others to enjoy. Social media, for all its flaws, can be a great venue for this, especially if there's nothing in your local community that suits your needs. There is no shortage of opportunities to find your audience in the age of the internet.

Sagittarians Are Blunt and Tactless

Honesty is the best policy, as they say, and frankly, it's a lot easier than remembering which lies you've told to which people. But in a lot of situations, truth bombs aren't welcome, or even necessary or useful—they're just cruel. Some people go around being rude unnecessarily, and try to cover for it by saying they're *just being honest.*

The Fix: Aim Your Truth Bombs Strategically

In my day job as a project manager, my team lead appreciates my ability to thoughtfully call out inefficiencies or bad processes to help us do our jobs better. And outside my professional life, I've found that there are a surprising number of occasions where somebody has to be the one to say "the Emperor has no clothes!" and, as a Sagittarius, I am exceptionally well suited to that task. We can direct our truth bombs toward situations where we can make a positive impact, rather than just flinging them willy-nilly at anyone we think needs to hear the Gospel According to Us. In the words of detective Benoit Blanc in the movie *Glass Onion*, "It's a dangerous thing to mistake speaking without thought for speaking the truth. Don't you think?"[8]

Sagittarians Are Capricious, Flaky, and Sleazy

Variety is the spice of life, and our Sagittarian open-minded nature leads us to explore all kinds of exotic and interesting things. It's part of what makes us charismatic, fun people to be around.

If our thirst for variety manifests in our romantic lives, however, we can be fickle and capricious, leaving our partners feeling hurt and used when we abandon them. For both monogamous and polyamorous Sagittarians, this may manifest

8. Rian Johnson, director, *Glass Onion: A Knives Out Mystery* (T-Street, 2022).

as an addiction to NRE (New Relationship Energy), where you're constantly chasing that high of a new relationship and ending relationships when they no longer provide it, even if it's otherwise a great relationship. You may even see this trend in your friendships or communities if you're always chasing the new and shiny people and community connections.

Sagittarians also have a bit of a reputation for being somewhat lecherous at times. We can be overindulgent in our flirting and pursuit of sexual partners to the point where people around us may start to get uncomfortable. (I have definitely had my moments with this, much to my embarrassment.)

The Fix: Be Honest and Kind, and Get Creative

If you're concerned that you may be coming off as sleazy or lecherous when you're at a social gathering, take a few minutes every now and then to read the room, and always back off when someone doesn't indicate interest. Nobody likes a creeper, and not every gathering is a speed dating opportunity.

If you struggle to maintain platonic, romantic, or sexual relationships over the long-term, that isn't necessarily a bad thing. Some people just don't like long-term relationships, and there's nothing wrong with that as long as you're clear with yourself and others about what you want. Here's an opportunity to use that classic Sagittarian honesty! By being up-front about what you want, you will avoid using people or leading them to expect more than you're willing to give.

(Of course, some people may not believe you, or they may believe they can change your mind. People and relationships are complicated!)

In addition to that, take some time to turn your Sagittarian knack for honesty inward. Some people secretly believe they don't deserve love or happiness and unconsciously self-sabotage relationships that look promising to keep feeding themselves a narrative of being unworthy. If you think this might be you, it's worth doing some thinking, and maybe talk to a therapist about it.

You can also use your natural Sagittarian creativity to envision how you want your life to be, and open your mind to unconventional possibilities. The so-called nuclear family structure is not the only option for how to live your life. In fact, it's entirely possible to have autonomy and independence while maintaining healthy, long-term relationships with romantic partners. I have had a few friends whose spouses live in different homes, cities, or even states, for example. If, like most Sagittarians, you crave a life that you can define while also cocreating parts of that life with another person or other people, you can work to make it so. Honesty, transparency, and thinking outside the proverbial box may lead you to a relationship structure that's a bit outside the norm, but works for you and your partner(s).

Your Sun Sign Is Not an Excuse

Blaming bad behavior on your Sun sign, believing that's just the way you are, is deeply limiting. You can embrace the energy of Sagittarius without being bound by it, and you can rise to Sagittarian potential without being dragged down by our less-great behaviors. If you believe you can't be or do something based on your Sun sign, you're wrong. If you've made mistakes in the past, you can learn from them and change how you approach similar situations in the future. As Ivo said earlier in this book, "You have the capacity to activate dormant traits, to shape functioning traits, and to tone down overactive traits." Astrology can liberate you to lean into your best qualities and seek opportunities to do and be more, if you use it well.

POSTCARD FROM A SAGITTARIUS WITCH

Cosette Paneque

I sat at the kitchen table while my mother braided my hair. We chatted with my sister, who flipped through the newest issue of Cosmopolitan. In the background, the radio played the news or the latest ballad by Luis Miguel. There was a break in the programming for Walter Mercado, the famous Puerto Rican astrologer. We hushed to listen.

"Sagitario, la verdad y la honestidad hecha carne. Los eternos peregrinos o viajeros. Siempre van o vienen de algún lugar."[9]

I didn't understand as a child, but I was always excited to hear him call out my sign and speak to me. Today, I know that Sagittarius is my core. Its qualities, characteristics, and symbols of mutable fire, the ruling planet Jupiter, and the archer centaur describe me, power my magick, and propel me.

Mutable fire is essential to my life and magick. It makes me adaptable and ready for change. It fuels my passionate pursuit of knowledge, courage, willpower, creativity, and power to transform. Fire is a favorite ritual vehicle, and I use it to help induce a trance state for scrying, banishing, cleansing, and, of course, candle magick.

9. "Sagittarius, truth and honesty made flesh. The eternal pilgrims or travelers. They are always coming or going from some location."

Jupiter, my ruling planet, feeds my spirit of exploration, is my fountain of optimism, and is why I land on my feet. It is why I could move from the United States to Australia or suddenly quit my job. She'll be right, as Aussies say.

Sagittarius, the constellation, is the archer centaur. His bow and arrow speak to the straightforward energy of the zodiac sign, but the centaur himself is an enigmatic being and a significant symbol for me.

Greek mythology depicts centaurs as wild, uncontrollable, with a taste for sex and chaos, the embodiment of untamed nature. However, some centaurs, such as Chiron and Pholos, were intelligent, kind, brave, loyal, and civilized. This duality is visible in the skies.

Sagittarius is the centaur sometimes described as a warrior because he's an archer pointing his arrow toward the star Antares, the heart of Scorpius, ready to attack. A second centaur in the sky, the constellation Centaurus, is associated with Chiron, the wise mentor of heroes.

The centaur is a liminal being. His half-human, half-horse composition shows he is between two states, nature and human civilization, and his human upper body represents his evolution. Like the centaur, Sagittarius is courageous,

impulsive, a little wild, and loves to run free. Sagittarius also seeks wisdom and spiritual evolution.

The centaur's liminality speaks to me. Witches walk between the worlds, and I am comfortable with ambiguity, able to manage disorientation, and can guide others through it. Whether I perform divination, worship at the crossroads, or provide deathcare, the centaur reminds me that the threshold is where some of my most meaningful experiences happen.

Our Sun Sign is the best place to discover a deep and personal source of our power and find direction. With so much to explore (glyphs, colors, symbols, and more), our Sun sign is where the journey begins, is the road map, and the destination.

SPIRIT OF SAGITTARIUS GUIDANCE RITUAL

Ivo Dominguez, Jr.

The signs are more than useful constructs in astrology or categories for describing temperaments, they are also powerful and complicated spiritual entities. So, what is meant when we say that a sign is a spirit? I often describe the signs of the zodiac as the twelve forms of human wisdom and folly. The signs are twelve styles of human consciousness, which also means that the signs are well-developed group minds and egregores. Think on the myriad of people over thousands of years who have poured energy into the constructs of the signs through intentional visualization and study. Moreover, the lived experience of each person as one of the signs is deposited into the group minds and egregores of their sign; they are ensouled. Every Sagittarius who has ever lived or is living contributes to the spirit of Sagittarius.

The signs have a composite nature that allows them to exist in many forms on multiple planes of reality at once. In addition to the human contribution to their existence, the spirits of the signs are made from inputs from all living beings in our world whether they are made of dense matter or spiritual substances. These vast and ancient thoughtforms that became group minds and then egregores are also vessels that can be used by divine beings to communicate with humans as well. The spirits of the signs can manifest themselves as small as a sprite or larger than the Earth. The shape and the magnitude of the spirit of Sagittarius emerging before you will depend on who you are and how and why you call upon them.

Purpose and Use

This ritual will make it possible to commune with the spirit of Sagittarius. The form that the spirit will take will be different each time you perform the ritual. What appears will be determined by what you are looking for and your state of mind and soul. The process for preparing yourself for the ritual will do you good as well. Exploring your circumstances, motivations, and intentions is a valuable experience whether or not you are performing this ritual.

If you have a practical problem you are trying to solve or an obstacle that must be overcome, the spirit of Sagittarius may have useful advice. If you are trying to better understand who you are and what you are striving to accomplish, then the spirit of Sagittarius can be your mentor. Should you have a need to recharge yourself or flush out stale energy, you can use this ritual to reconnect with a strong clear current of power. This energy can be used for magickal empowerment, physical vitality, or healing or redirected for spell work. If you are charging objects or magickal implements with Sagittarius energy, this ritual can be used for this purpose as well.

Timing for the Ritual

The prevailing astrological conditions have an impact on how you experience a ritual, the type and amount of power available, and the outcomes of the work. If you decide you want to go deeper in your studies of astrology, you'll find many techniques to pick the best day and time for your ritual. Thankfully, the ritual to meet the spirit of your sign does not require exact timing or perfect astrological conditions. This ritual depends on your inner connection to your Sun sign, so it is not as reliant on the external celestial conditions as some other rituals. Each of us has worlds within ourselves, which include inner landscapes and inner skies. Your birth chart, and the sky that it depicts, burns brightest within you. Although not required, you can improve the effectiveness of this ritual if you use any of the following simple guidelines for favorable times:

- When the Moon or the Sun is in Sagittarius.
- When Jupiter is in Sagittarius.
- On Thursday, the day of Jupiter, and even better at dawn, which is its planetary hour.
- When Jupiter is in Cancer, where it is exalted.

Materials and Setup

The following is a description of the physical objects that will make it easier to perform this ritual. Don't worry if you don't have all of them, as in a pinch, you need no props. However, the physical objects will help anchor the energy and your mental focus.

You will need:

- A printout of your birth chart
- A table to serve as an altar
- A chair if you want to sit during the ritual
- A candle, ideally a dark blue one but any color will do (for fire safety, it should be in glass and on a plate or tray)
- Items for the altar that correspond with Sagittarius or Jupiter (for example, a turquoise or an iolite, a gingerroot or nutmeg, and a cornflower or snapdragon)
- A pad and a pen or chalk and a small blackboard, or something else you can use to draw a glyph

Before beginning the ritual, you may wish to copy the ritual invocations onto paper or bookmark this chapter and bring the book into the ritual. I find that the process of writing out the invocation, whether handwritten or typed, helps forge a better connection with the words and their meaning. If possible, put the altar table in the center of your space, and if not, then as close to due east as you can manage. Light the candle and place it on the altar. Put the printout of your birth chart on the altar to one side of the candle and arrange the items you have selected to anchor the Sagittarius and Jupiter energy around it. To the other side of the candle, place the pad and pen. Make sure you turn off your phone, close the door, close the curtains, or do whatever else is needed to prevent distractions.

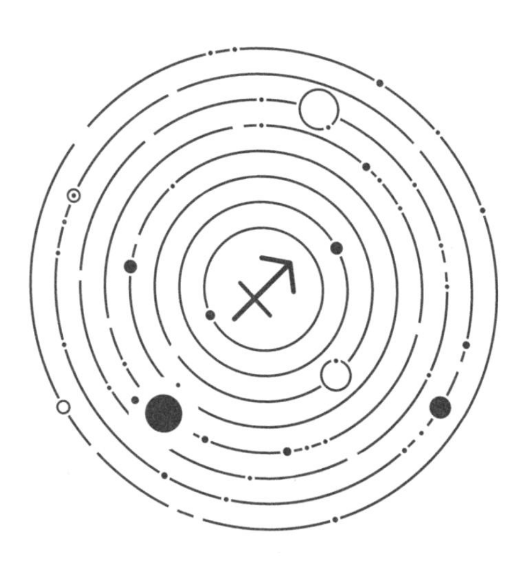

Ritual to Meet the Spirit of Your Sign

You may stand or be seated—whichever is most comfortable for you. Begin by focusing on your breathing. When you pay attention to the process of breathing, you become more aware of your body, the flow of your life energy, and the balance between conscious and unconscious actions. After you have done so for about a minute, it is time to shift into fourfold breathing. This consists of four phases: inhaling, lungs full, exhaling, and lungs empty. You count to keep time so that each of the four phases is of equal duration. Try a count of four or five in your first efforts. Depending on your lungs and how fast you count, you will need to adjust the number higher or lower. When you hold your breath, hold it with your belly muscles, not your throat. When you hold your breath in fourfold breathing, your throat should feel relaxed. Be gentle and careful with yourself if you have asthma, high blood pressure, are late in pregnancy, or have any other condition that may have an impact on your breathing and blood pressure. In general, if there are difficulties, they arise during the lungs' full or empty phases because of holding them by clenching the throat or compressing the lungs. The empty and the full lungs should be held by the position of the diaphragm, and the air passages left open. After one to three minutes of fourfold breathing, you can return to your normal breathing pattern.

Now, close your eyes and move your center of consciousness down into the middle of your chest. Proceed with grounding and centering, dropping and opening, shifting into the alpha state, or whatever practice you use to reach the state of mind that supports ritual work. Then gaze deeply inside yourself and see a fire. The flames can be in a hearth, a bonfire, on a torch, or whatever feels right to you. Look at the dancing flames, hear the crackling, and feel the warmth. Reach out from that central fire and awaken all the places and spaces within you that are of Sagittarius. When you feel ready, open your eyes.

Zodiac Casting

If you are seated, stand if you are able and face the east. Slowly read this invocation aloud, putting some energy into your words. As you read, slowly turn counterclockwise so that you come full circle when you reach the last line. Another option is to hold your hand over your head and trace the counterclockwise circle of the zodiac with your finger.

I call forth the twelve to join me in this rite.
I call forth Aries and the power of courage.
I call forth Taurus and the power of stability.
I call forth Gemini and the power of versatility.
I call forth Cancer and the power of protection.
I call forth Leo and the power of the will.
I call forth Virgo and the power of discernment.
I call forth Libra and the power of harmony.
I call forth Scorpio and the power of renewal.
I call forth Sagittarius and the power of vision.
I call forth Capricorn and the power of responsibility.
I call forth Aquarius and the power of innovation.
I call forth Pisces and the power of compassion.
The power of the twelve is here.
Blessed be!

Take a few deep breaths and gaze at the candle flame. Become aware of the changes in the atmosphere around you and the presence of the twelve signs.

Altar Work

Pick up the printout of your birth chart and look at your chart. Touch each of the twelve houses with your finger and push energy into them. You are energizing and awakening your birth chart to act as a focal point of power on the altar. Put your chart back on the altar when it feels ready to you. Then take the pad and pen and write the glyph for Sagittarius again and again. The glyphs can be different sizes, they can overlap; you can make any pattern with them you like so long as you pour energy into the ink as you write. Scribing the glyph is an action that helps draw the interest of the spirit of Sagittarius. Periodically look at the candle flame as you continue scribing the glyph. When you feel sensations in your body such as electric tingles, warmth, shivers, or something that you associate with the approach of a spirit, it is time to move on to the next step. If these are new experiences for you, just follow your instincts. Put away the pen and paper and pick up the sheet with the invocation of Sagittarius.

Invoking Sagittarius

Before beginning, think on what you hope to accomplish in this ritual and why it matters to you. Then speak these lines slowly and with conviction.

Sagittarius, hear me, for I am born in the dance of the mutable fire.
Sagittarius, see me, for the Sagittarius Sun shines upon me.
Sagittarius, know me as a member of your family and your company.
Sagittarius, know me as your student and your protégé.
Sagittarius, know me as a conduit for your power.
Sagittarius, know me as a wielder of your magick.
I am of you, and you are of me.
I am of you, and you are of me.
I am of you, and you are of me.
Sagittarius is here, within and without.
Blessed be!

Your Requests

Now, look at the candle for several deep breaths, and silently or aloud welcome the spirit of Sagittarius. Close your eyes and ask for any guidance that would be beneficial for you and listen. It may take some time before anything comes through, so be patient. I find it valuable to receive guidance before making a request so that I can refine or modify intentions and outcomes. Consider the meaning of whatever impressions or guidance you received and reaffirm your intentions and desired outcomes for this ritual.

It is more effective to use multiple modes of communication to make your request. Speak silently or aloud the words that describe your need and how it could be solved. Visualize the same message but without the words and project the images on your mind's screen. Then put all your attention on your feelings and your bodily sensations that have been stirred up by contemplating your appeal to the spirit of Sagittarius. Once again, wait and use all your physical and psychic senses to perceive what is given. At this point in the ritual, if there are objects to be charged, touch them or focus your gaze on them.

Offer Gratitude

You may be certain or uncertain about the success of the ritual or the time frame for the outcomes to become clear. Regardless of that, it is a good practice to offer thanks and gratitude to the spirit of Sagittarius for being present. Also, thank yourself for doing your part of the work. The state of heart and mind that comes with thanks and gratitude makes it easier for the work to become manifest. Thanks and gratitude also act as a buffer against the unintended consequences that can be put into motion by rituals.

Release the Ritual

If you are seated, stand if you are able and face the east. Slowly turn clockwise until you come full circle while repeating the following or something similar.

> *Return, return oh turning wheel to your*
> *starry home.*
> *Farewell, farewell oh Sagittarius wise until*
> *we speak again.*

Another option while saying these words is to hold your hand over your head and trace a clockwise circle of the zodiac with your finger. When you are done, snuff out the candle on the altar and say,

It is done. It is done. It is done.

Afterward

I encourage you to write down your thoughts and observations of what you experienced in the ritual. Do this while it is still fresh in mind before the details begin to blur. The information will become more useful over time as you work more with the spirit of Sagittarius. It will also let you evaluate the outcomes of your workings and improve your process in future workings. This note-taking or journaling will also help you dial in any changes or refinements to this ritual for future use. Contingent upon the guidance you received or the outcomes you desire, you may want to add reminders to your calendar.

More Options

These are some modifications to this ritual that you may wish to try:

- Put together or purchase Sagittarius incense to burn during the ritual. A Sagittarius oil to anoint the candle is another possibility. I'm providing one of my oil recipes as a possibility.
- Set up a richer and deeper altar. In addition to adding more objects that resonate to the energy of Sagittarius or Jupiter, consecrate each object before the ritual. You may also want to place an altar cloth on the table that brings to mind Sagittarius, Jupiter, or the element of fire.
- Creating a sigil to concentrate the essence of what you are working toward would be a good addition to the altar.
- Consider adding chanting, free-form toning, or movement to raise energy for the altar work and/or for invoking Sagittarius.

- If you feel inspired, you can write your own invocations for calling the zodiac and/or invoking Sagittarius. This is a great way to deepen your understanding of the signs and to personalize your ritual.

Rituals have greater personal meaning and effectiveness when you personalize them and make them your own.

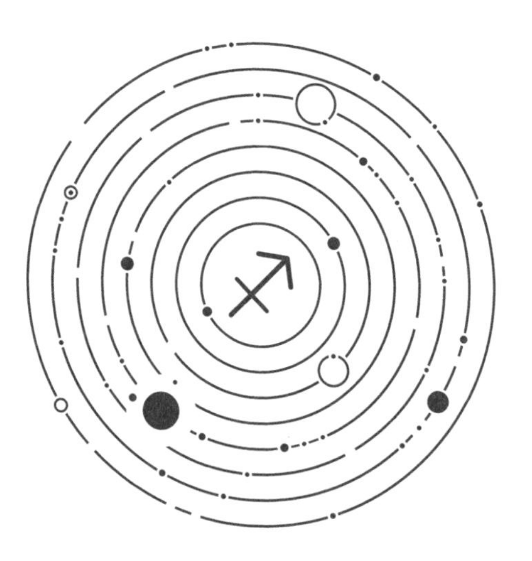

SAGITTARIUS ANOINTING OIL RECIPE

* * *

Ivo Dominguez, Jr.

This oil is used for charging and consecrating candles, crystals, and other objects you use in your practice. This oil makes it easier for an object to be imbued with Sagittarius energy. It also primes and tunes the objects so your will and power as a Sagittarius witch flow more easily into them. Do not apply the oil to your skin unless you have done an allergy test first.

Ingredients:

- Carrier oil—1 ounce
- Cedar—6 drops
- Rosewood—4 drops
- Frankincense—4 drops
- Star anise—4 drops
- Rose—2 drops

Instructions:

Pour one ounce of a carrier oil into a small bottle or vial. The preferred carrier oils are almond oil or fractionated coconut oil, but others can be used. Ideally use essential oils, but fragrance oils can be used as substitutes. Add the drops of the essential oils into the carrier oil. Once they have all been added, cap the bottle tightly, and shake the bottle several times. Hold the bottle in your hands, take a breath, and pour energy into the oil. Visualize royal blue energy, the glyph for Sagittarius, repeat the word *Sagittarius*, and raise energy in your preferred manner. Continue doing so until the oil feels warm, seems to glow, or you sense that it is charged.

Label the bottle and store the oil in a cool, dark place. Consider keeping a little bit of each previous batch of oil to add to the new batch. This helps build the strength and continuity of the energy and intentions you have placed in the oil. Over time, that link makes your oils more powerful.

BETTER EVERY DAY: THE WAY FORWARD

Enfys J. Book

So what's next? How can you embrace your Sagittarian qualities to become a better human and witch? The answer will differ depending on your unique circumstances and where you are on your journey, but I have several suggestions.

Give Your Natural Energy, Enthusiasm, and Passion a Container

Think about a steam engine. Two things are needed to make it work: you need the structure of the engine to force the steam to move the parts, and you need steam. If steam is released in a big room with no container, it doesn't do much. It doesn't even noticeably heat up the room. And the engine, with no steam, doesn't do anything, either. But if you direct that steam into the engine, a container in which to work, it can create power. The challenge for Sagittarian witches is to have enough focus to direct our vast amounts of energy to create things. And I know, the short-attention-span power is strong with us, so that's not an easy thing. Here are some exercises to increase your focus.

Meditate with a Candle

Breathe deeply and watch the flame. Focus on it. If you feel your attention drifting, gently return your attention to the flame and your breath. Start doing this for one minute a day, then increase it by one minute every week until you can focus for a few minutes. You can also use a meditation app that slowly strengthens your ability to focus over time.

Say a Prayer or Use a Daily Mantra

When you wake up in the morning, what is the first thing you do? Grab your phone and check your messages? Read the news? Try this instead: start your day with a prayer or mantra to remind yourself and the spirits you work with about your goal to increase your focus. Maybe light a stick of incense or a candle as well to give your senses a treat. It's best if you write the mantra yourself, but here are some starter ideas for you:

> *I am a focused being, powerful and capable of directing my boundless energy toward my goals.*

> *Quick of tongue and full of spark,*
> *I come to shine a light in the dark.*
> *Let my passion find focus and clarity,*

That my Will becomes manifest. So mote it be.

[Spirit or deity], I ask for your aid in helping me increase my focus, so that my natural passion can be put to good use.

Do Some Work with Jupiter

Jupiter is the ruling planet of Sagittarius, and its deity can teach us a lot. Jupiter, like Zeus in the Greek pantheon, is expansive and boisterous, prosperous, but also strategic, holding a lot of responsibility brokering peace among the other gods. And, interestingly, Jupiter provides cardinal energy that is beneficial to balance the mutable energy of Sagittarius. If you think of mutable energy as being a squishy egg that is always evolving and changing (okay, yes, you can think of it like a Pokémon, I'm not going to stop you), then cardinal energy is like a rocket launching: it is energy sent in a particular direction. It's the bow and arrow part of the Sagittarius centaur image. We're wild and passionate beings, but we're aiming to *do* something with all that energy and potential. Working with Jupiter can help you figure out where to point your arrow.

A Spell to Break Out of Stagnation

Even with all our fiery energy, sometimes we can get into a rut. Sagittarians don't do well with stagnation and boredom—they tend to bring out the worst in us. If you or a situation feels stuck, here's a spell that uses the mutable energy of Sagittarius to help you break free. For extra power, perform this spell on a new Moon.

You will need:

- A small piece of paper
- A pencil or pen to write with
- A small white tealight candle
- A butter knife, an old ballpoint pen, or another sharpish object to carve a symbol on the candle
- A fireproof vessel (a small cauldron or a cooking pot will work)
- A couple of drops of diluted orange or cinnamon essential oil (see note)
- A match or lighter

Instructions:

Write on the piece of paper the thing you need to change: the situation that feels stuck. Carve the Sagittarius symbol onto the candle. Push the energy of change into the candle as you carve. Put the candle into the fireproof vessel.

As you drip five drops of essential oil on the candle, say,

I charge this candle with the power to catalyze change.

As you light the candle, say,

Let this flame represent the forthcoming change.

Hold the small piece of paper you wrote on over the lit candle. As you carefully touch it to the flame, focus on and say *how* you want the situation to change, ending with,

As it is now, it shall no longer be.

Make sure the whole piece of paper is consumed in the fire. Let the candle burn down and dispose of the ashes from the paper once they've cooled.

Note: Orange essential oil works best if you're focusing on the positive side of the change; cinnamon is for when you're more like *burn the earth and salt the ashes around this situation.* It's important to dilute oil before using, particularly the cinnamon oil, as it can be very irritating to skin. Use one drop of the essential oil per ten milliliters of carrier oil. In a pinch, you can also sprinkle a little bit of powdered cinnamon from your kitchen spice cabinet over the candle, too.

Find People Who Can Get on Your Level and Work Together on a Goal

Even if you don't consider yourself an extrovert, even if you've had terrible experiences with group projects, I guarantee you can make something great, something even better than you could do alone, with the right group of folks. Maybe you don't have any witches in your area, but hey, the internet exists. There are plenty of groups who work together virtually across the world, and virtual and in-person conferences where you can find people who share your interests. Bring your sassy, smart, bombastic self to a group that needs and values a cheerleader, or, even better, a group of super competent people making shit happen and grooving on a similar vibe as you. Search around for Facebook groups, Discords, and other enclaves where witches might virtually gather, get a sense of the drama level (because who has the time for *that* nonsense?), consult your preferred divination tool, and really listen to what people are saying before you jump in. And this talk of group work leads me to the next idea...

Check Yourself Before You Wreck Yourself

One of our downfalls as Sagittarians is that we don't always think things through before heading in a direction. Like the Fool in the Major Arcana of the tarot, we leap before we look. Sometimes (surprisingly often), things work out for us, thanks to our natural charm and good luck. But leaping isn't the best way to approach *every* situation.

For example, if I were to sum up my life regrets, they would almost all fall under the category of "me and my big mouth." I talk fast, and I talk *a lot*. And sometimes I say things without thinking, and end up really hurting people's feelings, losing friendships, getting myself into fights I had no intention of starting, or lowering people's opinions of me by popping off something that seemed witty or funny at the time, but about two seconds later I realized it came out *really* badly and wasn't what I meant at all. But you can't un-say words that have been spoken, and sometimes apologies are not enough. The damage has been done.

So, what do you do? My best advice is to simply *take a breath*. Before you jump into something that seems like a good idea, before you spout off unsolicited advice, simply pause for a few seconds, and take a breath. You'd be amazed at how much damage I've *avoided* simply by pausing. I'm not even thinking anything in particular about what I should do when I pause and breathe, I just *pause and breathe*. And, usually, my brain catches up with my mouth, or my fingers on the keyboard, and I stay out of trouble. (Mostly.)

Celebrate Your Awesomeness

Sagittarians have so many fantastic qualities. Lean into your passions for exploration, learning, and teaching, which may manifest differently in each individual. I have so much passion and joy and enthusiasm to share with the world, so much drive to make this world a better place, and so many exciting things I want to try. I'm not afraid to live my life boldly and out loud, and I will fight for the things that matter to me. And I have my Sun sign to thank for a lot of that, as well as my willingness to lead with the qualities that make Sagittarians great. You can do the same, and you may be doing so already! Remember all the great things that make you *you* and acknowledge them regularly.

Tending the Flame

Michael G. Smith

Unlike the cardinal fire of Aries or the fixed fire of Leo, my Sagittarian fire tends to grow and ebb unless I pay closer attention to its maintenance. I discovered one quick way to grow my fire is to connect to the Three Worlds and their fires: the Lower, the Middle, and the Higher and my Three Selves.

First, create a physical fire in the Middle World. It can be a candle, a woodstove or fireplace, or a bonfire. Gaze upon that fire until its image is firm in the mind's eye. Closing your eyes draws that image of fire to the hearthstone or center within and establishes it firmly in that place. Establish that the hearthstone is the container, and that no energy is allowed to spill out without your desire.

Next, open your awareness to the fires burning deep within the Earth, the Lower World fires. Through your will, draw those fires up to your hearthstone, merging and blending it with the Middle World fire already burning there. See that flame grow brighter and more complex, with differing colors of fire growing and ebbing within.

Now, open your awareness to the fires burning high over your head, the Sun fire of the Upper World. Again, through your will, bring that fire down upon your center, combining it with the Middle and Lower World fires already burning there. Again, the hearth fire grows larger, brighter, and more powerful and colorful.

Let the energy build and flow for a time until you feel fully energized. This sensation is different for everyone and will be different every time you use the technique depending on where you are in the moment. When you reach this point, gently release the connection to the Earth fire and the Sun fire, retaining what you have blended upon the hearth for your use. Ensure that the connections are completely closed, and the merged fire is contained in the space. Allow your consciousness to return to its "normal" waking place, keeping a connection to the heart fire, and open your eyes.

The next step depends on what you wish to accomplish with this fire. Sometimes I allow the energy to flow gently and steadily out into my physical and energetic bodies, filling myself with the energy to accomplish the tasks of daily life. Occasionally I send part of that fire back into the candle to burn as an aid while I engage in other magickal, spiritual, or ritual work. I have pushed the energy into a cleared crystal—citrine is my favorite, though others will work as well—to carry as a talisman when traveling or faced with a difficult circumstance. I've used that energy to charge talismans and amulets for others' use.

As a Sag it is very easy for me to burn through my *fuel* as I pursue the things that interest and attract me. And yes, it is true I could reduce the number of interests, but there is no fun in that. For me, the more satisfying choice is to use the fires of the Worlds to reenergize my flame.

CONCLUSION

Ivo Dominguez, Jr.

No doubt, you are putting what you discovered in this book to use in your witchcraft. You may have a desire to learn more about how astrology and witchcraft fit together. One of the best ways to do this is to talk about it with other practitioners. Look for online discussions, and if there is a local metaphysical shop, check to see if they have classes or discussion groups. If you don't find what you need, consider creating a study group. Learning more about your own birth chart is also an excellent next step.

At some point, you may wish to call upon the services of an astrologer to give you a reading that is fine-tuned to your chart. There are services that provide not just charts but full chart readings that are generated by software. These are a decent tool and more economical than a professional astrologer, but they lack the finesse and intuition that only a person can offer. Nonetheless, they can be a good starting point. If you do decide to hire an astrologer to do your chart, shop around to find someone attuned to your spiritual needs. You may decide to learn enough astrology to read your own chart, and that will serve you for many reasons. However, most practitioners of a divinatory art will seek out another practitioner rather than read for themselves in important matters. It is hard to see some things when you are too attached to the outcomes.

If you find your interest in astrology and its effect on a person's relationship to witchcraft has been stimulated by this book, you may wish to read the other books in this series. Additionally, if you have other witches you work with, you'll find that knowing more about how they approach their craft will make your collective efforts more productive. Understanding them better will also help reduce conflicts or misunderstandings. The ending of this book is really the beginning of an adventure. Go for it.

APPENDIX

SAGITTARIUS CORRESPONDENCES

November 22/23–December 20/22

Symbol: ♐

Solar System: Jupiter

Seasons: Autumn

Celebration: Winter Solstice

Runes: Is, Jara, Rad

Element: Fire

Colors: Black, Blue (Dark, Royal, Sky), Gold, Orange, Purple, Red, Yellow

Energy: Yang

Chakras: Root, Solar Plexus, Brow

Number: 9

Tarot: Temperance, Wheel of Fortune

Trees: Beech, Birch, Cedar, Chestnut, Elder, Elm, Holly, Horse Chestnut, Juniper, Linden, Myrtle, Oak, Palm (Dragon's Blood), Rowan, Spruce (Black)

Herb and Garden: Aster, Carnation, Clover (Red), Daffodil, Honeysuckle, Mugwort, Rose, Rosemary, Sage, St. John's Wort, Vervain

Miscellaneous Plants: Anise, Burdock, Clove, Deer's Tongue, Frankincense, Ginger, Nutmeg, Reed, Star Anise

Gemstones and Minerals: Amber, Amethyst, Azurite, Emerald, Herkimer Diamond, Iolite, Jasper (Brown, Yellow), Labradorite, Lapis Lazuli, Obsidian, Opal, Peridot, Ruby, Sapphire (Star), Sodalite, Sphene, Spinel, Sugilite, Topaz, Tourmaline (Black, Green, Red), Turquoise, Zircon (Red)

Metals: Tin

Goddesses: Anat, Artemis, Athena, Diana, Epona, Isis, Rhiannon

Gods: Hades, Jupiter, Mars, Nergal, Thor

Angel: Michael

Animals: Deer (Doe), Elk, Horse, Lion, Monkey

Issues, Intentions, and Powers: Beauty, Consciousness, Danger, Dreamwork, Energy, Enlightenment, Fear, Freedom, Growth, Honesty, Improvement, Independence, Intuition, Knowledge, Leadership (Ability), Magic (Animal), Optimism, Prophecy, Self-Work, Sexuality, Spirituality, Travel, Truth, Unity

RESOURCES

Online

Astrodienst: Free birth charts and many resources.

- https://www.astro.com/horoscope

Astrolabe: Free birth chart and software resources.

- https://alabe.com

The Astrology Podcast: A weekly podcast hosted by professional astrologer Chris Brennan.

- https://theastrologypodcast.com

Magazine

The world's most recognized astrology magazine (available in print and digital formats).

- https://mountainastrologer.com

Books

- *Practical Astrology for Witches and Pagans* by Ivo Dominguez, Jr.
- *Parkers' Astrology: The Definitive Guide to Using Astrology in Every Aspect of Your Life by* Julia and Derek Parker

- *The Inner Sky: How to Make Wiser Choices for a More Fulfilling Life* by Steven Forrest
- *Predictive Astrology: Tools to Forecast Your Life and Create Your Brightest Future* by Bernadette Brady
- *Chart Interpretation Handbook: Guidelines for Understanding the Essentials of the Birth Chart* by Stephen Arroyo
- *Twist Your Fate: Manifest Success with Astrology and Tarot* by Theresa Reed (Weiser, 2022)
- *Make Magic of Your Life: Passion, Purpose, and the Power of Desire* by T. Thorn Coyle (Weiser, 2013)

Sources Consulted for Dion Fortune Bio

- Chapman, Janine. *The Quest for Dion Fortune*. York Beach, ME: Samuel Weiser, 1993.
- Collins, Carr, and Charles Fielding. *The Story of Dion Fortune*. Leicestershire, UK: Thoth Publications, 1998.
- Richardson, Alan. *20th Century Magic and the Old Religion*. Woodbury, MN: Llewellyn Publications, 1991.

CONTRIBUTORS

We give thanks and appreciation to all our guest authors who contributed their own special Sagittarius energy to this project.

Donyelle Headington

Donyelle Headington is a folk magick practitioner, ancestor specialist, and Culture Bearer in Minneapolis, Minnesota. She carries the lineages of Afrocentric Kemetism, the Völva path, and Curanderismo, using these traditions to serve her communities as reader, healer, and community "Auntie." She can be contacted at www.sisterd.com.

Dawn Aurora Hunt

Dawn Aurora Hunt, owner of Cucina Aurora Kitchen Witchery, is the author of *A Kitchen Witch's Guide to Love & Romance* and *Kitchen Witchcraft for Beginners*. Though not born under the sign of Sagittarius, she combines knowledge of spiritual goals and magickal ingredients to create recipes for all Sun signs in this series. She is a Scorpio. Find her at www.CucinaAurora.com.

Devin Hunter

Devin Hunter is an award-winning and bestselling author, presenter, and occultist. His AV Club– and Cosmo-recommended podcast, *Modern Witch,* celebrated ten years in 2022, and his works have been featured on television shows like ABC's *To Tell the Truth.* Find out more about Devin at www.modernwitch.com.

Sandra Kynes

Sandra Kynes (Midcoast Maine) is the author of seventeen books, including *Mixing Essential Oils for Magic, Magical Symbols and Alphabets, Crystal Magic, Plant Magic,* and *Sea Magic.* Excerpted content from her book, *Llewellyn's Complete Book of Correspondences,* has been used throughout this series, and she is a Scorpio. Find her at http://www.kynes.net.

Mama Gina

A true Sagittarius, Mama Gina is a full-time touring Bard from Tampa, Florida. She shares her music, magick, and fearless storytelling throughout the United States, telling truth and singing of our responsibility to nurture both the mundane and the Divine. Connect with her at www.mamaginamusic.com.

Cosette Paneque

Cosette Paneque is a Sagittarius with Moon in Cancer and Scorpio Rising. She's also a Georgian Wiccan, a daughter of Ogun, an End-of-Life Doula, and a writer. Born in Havana and raised in Miami, she resides in Melbourne, Australia. Visit her at www.cosettepaneque.com.

Michael G. Smith

Michael G. Smith has practiced Wicca and esoteric disciplines since 1989. He became a member of the Assembly of the Sacred Wheel in 1993. He is an Elder of the ASW and served as High Priest of two of its covens. He lives with his husbands on Seelie Court, Pagan-owned land in Southern Delaware.

Natalie Zaman

Natalie Zaman is the author of the award-winning books *Magical Destinations of the Northeast* and *Color and Conjure* (Llewellyn) and is a regular contributor to Llewellyn's annual anthologies. She lives in New Jersey with her family.

Notes

Notes

Notes

Notes

Notes

To Write to the Author

If you wish to contact the author or would like more information about this book, please write to the author in care of Llewellyn Worldwide Ltd. and we will forward your request. Both the author and the publisher appreciate hearing from you and learning of your enjoyment of this book and how it has helped you. Llewellyn Worldwide Ltd. cannot guarantee that every letter written to the author can be answered, but all will be forwarded. Please write to:

Ivo Dominguez, Jr.
Enfys J. Book
℅ Llewellyn Worldwide
2143 Wooddale Drive
Woodbury, MN 55125-2989

Please enclose a self-addressed stamped envelope for reply, or $1.00 to cover costs. If outside the U.S.A., enclose an international postal reply coupon.

Many of Llewellyn's authors have websites with additional information and resources. For more information, please visit our website at:

www.llewellyn.com